Ctrl + Shift + Frontend

Welcome to the exciting world of Frontend Development, where websites come to life with a dash of code and creativity! This book is your trusty sidekick as you dive into the essentials—HTML, CSS, and JavaScript—and explore the wonders of modern frameworks like React and Angular. We'll guide you through the basics of building sleek, responsive websites that work on all devices (yes, even your grandma's tablet!). You'll learn how to make your sites super fast and easy to use, all while avoiding the headache of TypeScript (we're keeping it simple here!). Whether you're starting from square one or brushing up on the basics, this book is perfect for anyone ready to jump into the front-end world and build some cool stuff!

Ctrl + Shift + Frontend

To my younger self who would have loved this as a starting point.

ACKNOWLEDGEMENT

First, to the incredible teachers who pushed me, challenged me, and never let me settle for anything less than my best. You planted the seeds that led me here, and for that, I'm forever grateful. To my mom and family, who supported me through every bug, late night, and crazy idea. Your love and belief in me kept me going, even when my code didn't. You are my foundation.

A big thanks to the modern holy grail of developers: Google, Stack Overflow, GitHub, and YouTube. You built the bedrock of my coding knowledge and never judged me for searching the same question five times in a row. To my friends, who not only helped me become a better programmer but also sat with me debugging for hours—sometimes with snacks, sometimes with frustration, but always with support. You're the real MVPs of my coding journey.

To life, for teaching me lessons the hard way—because easy mode isn't a thing in reality or in code. To coding itself, my constant companion and sometimes nemesis. Thanks for keeping me on my toes, and letting me create things that I'm actually proud of. A huge thank you to the open-source community, whose tireless work and generous spirit made this journey possible. Without you, the coding world wouldn't be the collaborative space it is today.

To my team at Aivirex Innovations, thank you for being the spark that pushed me to start writing this book. Your brilliance and drive (and need for a good learning resource!) made this whole project come to life. And to my incredible interns—you made this all worth it.

Hrithika R, my coauthor, thank you for your patience and for putting up with me while we worked on this book together. You balanced out my quirks and made this project so much better.

Lastly, to myself: you did it. You didn't give up. You pushed through the doubts, the long nights, and the endless "one last feature" moments. This one's for you.

ABOUT THE AUTHORS

I'm K Sai Anirudh, the founder of Aivirex Innovations LLP, a tech-based startup dedicated to addressing issues that the majority of the population encounters with the help of innovation and technology. I hold a Master's degree in AI and Data Science, and I am passionate about combining my expertise in technology with education to create engaging and accessible learning experiences for young minds.

I'm Hrithika R,

Our mission is to make complex subjects approachable and enjoyable, sparking curiosity and fostering a love of learning while inspiring the next generation of tech innovators.

Follow us on social media to stay updated on my latest books and educational initiatives. Let's inspire the next generation of tech innovators together!

Ctrl + Shift + Frontend

TABLE OF CONTENT

Topics	Page No.
Acknowledgement	3
About the authors	4
Table of Content	5
Introduction	6
Chapter 1 - HTML	7
Chapter 2 - CSS	26
Chapter 3 - Version Control and CSS Framework	45
Chapter 4 - JavaScript	57
Chapter 5 - Frontend Frameworks	78
Note to Readers	121

Ctrl + Shift + Frontend

INTRODUCTION

Hey guys, welcome to our 5-chapter frontend web development book! Over the next 5 chapters, we're going to cover everything you need to know to build beautiful, responsive websites and web applications. Feel free to scan the QR code and follow along with the coding process. It contains a curated collection of valuable links and references to enhance your learning experience.

Did you know that over 4.6 billion people use the internet worldwide? That means there's a huge demand for talented frontend developers who can create engaging, user-friendly web experiences. In Chapter 1, we'll start with the basics of web development and HTML, the building blocks of the web. In Chapter 2, we'll dive into CSS, the styling language that brings HTML to life.

In Chapter 3, we'll let you choose your preferred CSS framework, either Tailwind or Bootstrap, and also cover the basics of version control using Git and GitHub.

Chapter 4 is all about JavaScript, the programming language that adds interactivity and dynamic functionality to web pages.

Finally, in Chapter 5, we'll introduce you to a frontend framework of your choice - either React or Angular - to help you build powerful, modern web applications. We're excited to help you become a skilled frontend developer and take your first steps towards a rewarding career in web development. Let's get started!

We know your time is valuable, which is why we've designed this book to fit your busy schedule. Each chapter, you'll learn new concepts and spend 1 to 3 hours a day mastering them. Then you'll apply what you've learned by completing a project, so don't forget to code along !

Consistency is key when it comes to coding and learning . Make an effort to read the book every day - even if it's just a little bit each day - and you'll be amazed at how much you can accomplish. We're excited to help you become a skilled frontend developer and we can't wait to see the amazing projects you'll create!

CHAPTER 1

Introduction to the Web

The Internet is a global network of computers and servers that communicate with each other using standardized communication protocols. It works by sending and receiving data packets between devices connected to the network. Each device is assigned a unique address, known as an IP address, which is used to identify the device and ensure that the data is sent to the correct destination.

To access the Internet, a device needs to be connected to a network that is connected to the Internet. This can be done through various means, such as wired and wireless connections, broadband, and satellite connections.

The Internet uses a suite of protocols called TCP/IP to facilitate communication between devices. TCP is responsible for breaking up large data packets into smaller pieces, while IP is responsible for routing these packets to their destination.

Overall, the Internet is a complex system that involves many different technologies working together to provide a seamless user experience. By understanding how it works, we can better appreciate the power of this incredible tool and the impact it has on our daily lives.

Introduction to HTML

Have you ever wondered what websites are made of? Well, it all starts with a language called HTML, or Hypertext Markup Language. It's like the building blocks of the web!

HTML allows us to structure content and add meaning to it, making it easily readable by both humans and computers. It's like giving instructions to a web browser on how to display our content.

HTML is made up of a bunch of tags, which are like little codes that tell the browser how to format and display our content. For example, we use tags like "<h1>" for headings, "<p>" for paragraphs, and "<img>" for images. It's like playing a game of tag with your web browser!

But don't worry, you don't need any fancy tools to create an HTML page. All you need is a simple text editor and a web browser. You just write the HTML code in the text editor, save the file with a .html extension, and open it in a web browser to see the results.

Choosing a Text Editor

When it comes to writing HTML code, you don't necessarily need a fancy text editor. A basic notepad can do the job, but it's much easier and efficient to use a text editor that's specifically designed for coding. One of the most popular text editors for web development is Visual Studio Code, which is free and available for Windows, Mac, and Linux. It's lightweight, customizable, and comes with a range of features that make coding a lot easier, such as syntax highlighting, code completion, and Git integration.

Other popular text editors for web development include Sublime Text, Atom, and Notepad++. Sublime Text is a paid text editor, but it offers a free trial period. Atom and Notepad++ are both free and available for Windows and Mac.

No matter which text editor you choose, make sure to download it from the official website to avoid any security issues. Once you have your text editor set up, you'll be ready to start coding HTML like a pro!

Creating a HTML File

To create an HTML file, you will need to use a text editor to create and edit your code. Once you've chosen a text editor, you can start by creating a new file and giving it an appropriate name with the .html extension, for example, index.html.

Next, you can start writing your HTML code within the file. HTML code is made up of different tags and elements that define the structure and content of your webpage.
To get started, you can begin with the basic structure of an HTML file, which is as follows:

Here, <!DOCTYPE html> is a declaration that tells the browser that the file is an HTML5 document. The <html> tag marks the beginning and end of the HTML document. The <head> tag contains information about the document, such as the title of the page, which is displayed in the browser's title bar. The <body> tag contains the content of the document, such as text, images, and links.

Once you have created your HTML file, you can save it and open it in a web browser to see how it looks. This is a great way to test your code and make sure it's working as expected.

Basic HTML Elements

The webpages we see are structured and made with a few elements, these elements have some attributes, the following are the list of html elements

- <!DOCTYPE html>: This tag defines the document type and should be placed at the beginning of every HTML document. It tells the web browser what version of HTML is being used and ensures that the document is displayed correctly.
- <html>: This tag represents the root element of an HTML document and encloses all other elements. It is used to define the document structure and to provide a container for all other HTML elements.

- <head>: This tag contains information about the document such as the title, links to external stylesheets, and metadata. It is used to define the head section of an HTML document.
- <title>: This tag defines the title of the document that appears in the browser tab. It is used to provide a title for the web page, which is displayed in the browser's title bar and is used by search engines to identify the page.
- <body>: This tag contains the content of the document such as text, images, and other elements. It is used to define the body section of an HTML document and to provide a container for all visible content on the page.
- <h1> to <h6>: These tags define headings of different levels. They are used to structure the content of a web page and to provide a hierarchical organization of headings.
- <p>: This tag defines a paragraph of text. It is used to separate blocks of text and to make the content more readable.
- <a>: This tag defines a hyperlink to another web page or a file. It is used to create clickable links that allow users to navigate between web pages.
- <img>: This tag defines an image and is used to display images on a web page. The src attribute is used to specify the image file.
- <ul> and <li>: These tags are used to create an unordered list. The <ul> tag represents the list and the <li> tag represents the list item. They are used to present a list of items in a way that is easy to read and understand.

```html
<!DOCTYPE html>
<html>
    <head>
        <title>Aivirex Innovations</title>
    </head>
    <body>
        <h1>Welcome to Frontend Development</h1>
        <p>This is some sample text.</p>
        <a href="https://aivirex.in">Click here</a> to visit Aivirex Website.
        <br>
        <img src="image.jpg" alt="A beautiful image">
        <ul>
            <li>List item 1</li>
            <li>List item 2</li>
            <li>List item 3</li>
        </ul>
    </body>
</html>
```

Ctrl + Shift + Frontend

Link and Anchor Tag

The <a> tag in HTML stands for "anchor" and is used to create hyperlinks to other web pages, files, email addresses, and more. Here are some of the ways in which you can use the <a> tag:

Link to Another Web Page:

To create a link to another web page, you can use the <a> tag with the "href" attribute that specifies the URL of the page you want to link to. Here's an example:

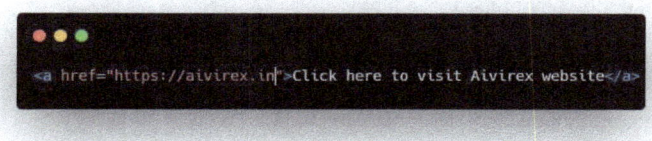

Link to an Email Address:

To create a link to an email address, you can use the <a> tag with the "href" attribute followed by "mailto:" and the email address you want to link to. Here's an example:

To create a link to a file, you can use the <a> tag with the "href" attribute that specifies the file path or URL. Here's an example:

Some of the commonly used attributes of the <a> tag are:

- **href**: Specifies the URL or file path to link to.
- **target**: Specifies where to open the linked document. "_blank" will open the document in a new window or tab, while "_self" will open the document in the same frame as it was clicked.
- **download**: Specifies that the linked document should be downloaded instead of opened in the browser.

In this code, we have used the following ways of using the <link> tag:

- To link an external stylesheet: <link rel="stylesheet" href="style.css">. This is used to apply styles to the page from an external CSS file.
- To link a favicon: <link rel="icon" href="favicon.ico">. This is used to specify the icon that appears in the browser tab.
- To link an RSS feed: <link rel="alternate" type="application/rss+xml" href="rss.xml" title="My RSS Feed">. This is used to specify the RSS feed for the page.
- To define inline styles: <style>/* CSS styles defined here will be applied only to this page */</style>. This is used to define styles that will be applied only to this page and not to any other page.

```
<!DOCTYPE html>
<html>
<head>
  <meta charset="UTF-8">
  <title>My Page</title>
  <link rel="stylesheet" href="style.css">
  <link rel="icon" href="favicon.ico">
  <link rel="alternate" type="application/rss+xml" href="rss.xml" title="My RSS Feed">
  <style>
    /* CSS styles defined here will be applied only to this page */
  </style>
</head>
<body>
  <h1>Welcome to My Page</h1>
  <p>This is the content of my page.</p>
</body>
</html>
```

Image

The image tag, or <img>, is used to add images to an HTML document. The tag is a self-closing tag, which means it doesn't have a closing tag. Instead, it uses attributes to specify the image source, alternative text, width, height, and more.

Here is an example of an <img> tag:

```
<img src="image.jpg" alt="A beautiful sunset" width="500" height="300">
<!-- alternatively we can use a link from the web -->
<img src="https://aivirex.in/assets/img/logo.png" alt="Logo of Aivirex" width="500" height="300">
```

In this example, we have used the following attributes:

- src: This specifies the source of the image. You can use either a relative or an absolute URL to specify the source. In this example, we have used a relative URL to specify the source as "image.jpg".
- alt: This specifies an alternative text for the image. This is important for accessibility, as it allows screen readers to read a description of the image to visually impaired users. In this example, we have used "A beautiful sunset" as the alternative text.
- width and height: These attributes specify the width and height of the image in pixels. In this example, we have set the width to 500 pixels and the height to 300 pixels.
- You can also use other attributes, such as title, class, and id, to further customize the image.

Videos

To embed a video into an HTML page, we can use the <video> tag. This tag allows us to specify the source of the video using the src attribute and set other attributes such as the width, height, and controls.

Here is an example code for embedding a video:

```html
<video src="video.mp4" width="640" height="360" autoplay loop muted poster="poster.jpg">
    Your browser does not support the video tag.
</video>
```

In the above code, the video will start playing automatically and will continue to play on a loop without sound. The poster attribute specifies an image to be displayed while the video is downloading or until the user hits the play button. If the browser does not support the <video> tag, the message "Your browser does not support the video tag." will be displayed.

The width and height attributes set the dimensions of the video player on the page.

Some other attributes that can be used with the <video> tag are:

- **autoplay**: The video will start playing automatically when the page loads.
- **loop**: The video will play on a loop until stopped.
- **muted**: The video will play without sound.
- **poster**: Specifies an image to be displayed while the video is downloading or until the user hits the play button.

Lists

HTML provides two types of lists: ordered lists and unordered lists. Both types of lists use the <ul> and <li> tags to define the list and list items, respectively.
The unordered list (<ul>) tag is used to create a bullet point list where the order of the list items doesn't matter. The <li> tag is used to define each item in the list. Here's an example:

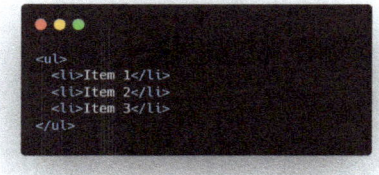

The ordered list (<ol>) tag is used to create a numbered list where the order of the list items does matter. The <li> tag is used to define each item in the list, just like in an unordered list. Here's an example:

Both the <ul> and <ol> tags have attributes that can be used to modify their appearance or behavior. Here are a few commonly used attributes:

- **type**: Used to change the type of bullets or numbering used in the list. For example, type="disc" will display a filled circle as the bullet point, while type="1" will display numbers as the list item markers.
- **start**: Used to specify the starting number for an ordered list. For example, start="3" will start the list items at 3 instead of 1.
- **reversed**: Used to reverse the order of an ordered list. For example, reversed will display the list items in reverse order (from highest number to lowest) instead of the usual order.

Tables

HTML tables are used to display data in rows and columns. They are a great way to organize information in a structured manner. To create a table, we use the <table> element.

The basic structure of an HTML table is as follows:

```
<table border="1">
    <tr>
        <th rowspan="2">Header 1</th>
        <th colspan="2">Header 2</th>
    </tr>
    <tr>
        <th>Subheader 1</th>
        <th>Subheader 2</th>
    </tr>
    <tr>
        <td>Row 1, Column 1</td>
        <td>Row 1, Column 2</td>
        <td>Row 1, Column 3</td>
    </tr>
    <tr>
        <td>Row 2, Column 1</td>
        <td>Row 2, Column 2</td>
        <td>Row 2, Column 3</td>
    </tr>
</table>
```

Here, we have used the <table> element to define the table. Inside the table, we have used the <tr> element to define a row. Inside the row, we have used the <th> element to define the header cells, and the <td> element to define the data cells. The th element is used to define header cells and the td element is used to define data cells.

Here, we have used the rowspan attribute to merge the first two cells in the first column, and the colspan attribute to merge the next two cells in the second row. The border attribute has been used to set the width of the table border.

Divs and Spans

A <div> tag is a container that groups together other HTML elements and applies styling to them as a group. It is used to organize content on a web page and make it easier to style with CSS. Here's an example:

```
<div>
    <h1>Welcome to my website!</h1>
    <p>Here you'll find all sorts of interesting content.</p>
    <ul>
        <li>Blog posts</li>
        <li>Product reviews</li>
        <li>Tutorials</li>
    </ul>
</div>
```

In the above example, the <div> tag contains a heading, a paragraph, and an unordered list. The contents of the <div> tag can be styled as a group using CSS. We will work more with this when we get to the CSS part.

A <span> tag is similar to a <div> tag, but it is used to group together smaller sections of content within a larger block of text. It is used when you want to apply styling to a small section of text within a larger block of text. Here's an example:

```
<p>Welcome to my website! Here you'll find all sorts of <span>interesting</span> content.</p>
```

In the above example, the word "interesting" is contained within a <span> tag. This allows you to apply CSS styles specifically to that word, without affecting the rest of the paragraph.

User Inputs

Input elements are used to create various types of form controls such as text boxes, buttons, checkboxes, radio buttons, and more. These controls can be used to collect user input or to trigger an action.

Text input:

The text input type creates a single-line input field for the user to enter text.

Attributes:

- type (required)
- name (optional)
- value (optional)
- placeholder (optional)
- maxlength (optional)
- required (optional)

Password input:

The password input type is used to create a single-line input field for the user to enter a password.

Attributes:

- type (required)
- name (optional)
- placeholder (optional)
- maxlength (optional)
- required (optional)

Email input:

The email input type is used to create a single-line input field for the user to enter an email address.

Attributes:

- type (required)
- name (optional)
- value (optional)
- placeholder (optional)
- maxlength (optional)
- required (optional)

Ctrl + Shift + Frontend

Number input:

The number input type is used to create a single-line input field for the user to enter a numeric value.

Attributes:

- type (required)
- name (optional)
- value (optional)
- min (optional)
- max (optional)
- step (optional)
- required (optional)

Checkbox input:

The checkbox input type creates a checkbox that the user can select or deselect.

Attributes:

- type (required)
- name (optional)
- value (optional)
- checked (optional)

Radio input:

The radio input type creates a radio button that the user can select. Radio buttons are grouped by name so that only one button in the group can be selected at a time.

Attributes:

- type (required)
- name (required)
- value (optional)
- checked (optional)

Select input:

The select input type creates a dropdown list of options for the user to choose from.

Attributes:

- name (optional)
- multiple (optional)
- size (optional)
- required (optional)

File input:

The file input type allows the user to select a file from their device to be uploaded.

Attributes:

- type (required)
- name (optional)
- accept (optional)
- required (optional)

Button input:

The button input type creates a button that can be used to trigger an action.

Attributes:

- type (required)
- name (optional)
- value (optional)

Submit input:

The submit input type creates a button that, when clicked, submits the form data to a server.

Ctrl + Shift + Frontend

Attributes:

- type (required)
- name (optional)
- value (optional)

Here is an example that demonstrates how to use some of these input types:

```html
<form>
    <label for="text-input">Text Input:</label>
    <input type="text" id="text-input" name="text-input"><br><br>

    <label for="password-input">Password Input:</label>
    <input type="password" id="password-input" name="password-input"><br><br>

    <label for="number-input">Number Input:</label>
    <input type="number" id="number-input" name="number-input"><br><br>

    <label for="range-input">Range Input:</label>
    <input type="range" id="range-input" name="range-input"><br><br>

    <label for="email-input">Email Input:</label>
    <input type="email" id="email-input" name="email-input"><br><br>

    <label for="date-input">Date Input:</label>
    <input type="date" id="date-input" name="date-input"><br><br>

    <label for="time-input">Time Input:</label>
    <input type="time" id="time-input" name="time-input"><br><br>

    <label for="checkbox-input">Checkbox Input:</label>
    <input type="checkbox" id="checkbox-input" name="checkbox-input" value="checkbox"><br><br>

    <label for="radio-input1">Radio Input 1:</label>
    <input type="radio" id="radio-input1" name="radio-input" value="radio1"><br><br>

    <label for="radio-input2">Radio Input 2:</label>
    <input type="radio" id="radio-input2" name="radio-input" value="radio2"><br><br>

    <label for="file-input">File Input:</label>
    <input type="file" id="file-input" name="file-input"><br><br>

    <label for="submit-input">Submit Input:</label>
    <input type="submit" id="submit-input" name="submit-input"><br><br>

    <label for="reset-input">Reset Input:</label>
    <input type="reset" id="reset-input" name="reset-input"><br><br>

    <label for="color-input">Color Input:</label>
    <input type="color" id="color-input" name="color-input"><br><br>

    <label for="search-input">Search Input:</label>
    <input type="search" id="search-input" name="search-input"><br><br>
</form>
```

Meta Tags

Meta tags are used to provide information about the HTML document that isn't visible on the web page. They are placed in the head section of an HTML document and are used by search engines and other services to provide information about the website or webpage.

```html
<!DOCTYPE html>
<html>
  <head>
    <meta charset="UTF-8">
    <meta name="description" content="This is a description of the webpage.">
    <meta name="keywords" content="HTML, CSS, JavaScript">
    <meta name="viewport" content="width=device-width, initial-scale=1.0">
    <meta http-equiv="content-type" content="text/html; charset=UTF-8">
    <title>My Webpage</title>
  </head>
  <body>
    <h1>Welcome to my webpage!</h1>
    <p>This is some content on my webpage.</p>
  </body>
</html>
```

There are several different types of meta tags, each with their own attributes and uses:

- **<meta charset>:** This tag is used to specify the character encoding used in the document. The most commonly used character encoding is UTF-8.
- **<meta name="description">:** This tag is used to provide a brief description of the content on the web page. This description is often displayed in search engine results.
- **<meta name="keywords">:** This tag is used to specify a list of keywords or phrases that are relevant to the content on the web page. This can help with search engine optimization.
- **<meta name="viewport">:** This tag is used to specify how the web page should be displayed on different devices. It is particularly useful for responsive web design.
- **<meta http-equiv>:** This tag is used to provide information about the document's HTTP headers, such as the content type and language.

Ctrl + Shift + Frontend

Chapter 1 Project

Instructions:

- Create a new HTML file and save it as "mypage.html".
- Add the <!DOCTYPE html> declaration to the beginning of the file to specify that this is an HTML document.
- Use the <html> tag to enclose all the other elements.
- Use the <head> tag to include the title of the webpage using the <title> tag.
- Use the <body> tag to include all the content of the webpage.
- Add a heading to the page using the <h1> tag with the title of the webpage.
- Create a paragraph about yourself using the <p> tag.
- Add an image to the page using the <img> tag. You can use an image of yourself or anything related to your webpage.
- Add a hyperlink to your favorite website using the <a> tag.
- Create an unordered list using the <ul> and <li> tags. Include at least three items in the list related to the content of your webpage.
- Create a table using the <table>, <tr>, <th>, and <td> tags. Include at least three rows and three columns with any data you like.
- Use the <div> and <span> tags to group related content.
- Add a video to your page using the <video> tag. You can use any video from YouTube or other video-sharing sites.
- Use user inputs like <input>, <textarea>, <select>, <option>, etc. to create a form where visitors can send feedback or messages to you.
- Use meta tags to add keywords and description to your webpage using <meta> tag.

Ctrl + Shift + Frontend

Notes:

- Make sure to properly close all tags.
- Use appropriate attributes for each tag to customize the display or behavior.
- Use the proper hierarchy of headings, paragraphs, and lists to organize the content.
- Make sure to use only HTML and not include any CSS or JavaScript in this project.
  Good luck with your project!

CHAPTER 2

Introduction to CSS

Welcome to the colorful world of CSS! It's like a big box of crayons, except instead of drawing on paper, we're painting styles on a webpage. With CSS, you can make your website look snazzy, stylish, and totally unique. It's like giving your website a new outfit every day, without ever having to go shopping. So let's get started and unleash our inner Picasso!

CSS (Cascading Style Sheets) and SCSS (Sassy CSS) are both used to style HTML documents. The primary difference between the two is the syntax used to write them.

CSS is a standard stylesheet language used to describe the presentation of an HTML document. It uses simple syntax and is written in plain text. CSS stylesheets consist of rulesets, which contain selectors that target specific HTML elements, and declarations that specify the styles to be applied to those elements.

SCSS, on the other hand, is a superset of CSS. It uses a more powerful and flexible syntax that includes features such as variables, nesting, and mixins. SCSS code is then compiled into standard CSS that the browser can understand. This allows for more efficient and organized stylesheet development, as well as the ability to reuse and share code across multiple stylesheets.

In summary, CSS is a standard stylesheet language with a simple syntax, while SCSS is a more powerful and flexible superset of CSS that must be compiled into standard CSS before it can be used in a web page.

How to add CSS

There are three ways to add CSS to an HTML document. These are:

Inline CSS: Inline CSS is used to apply styles directly to a single HTML element. To apply inline styles, you need to use the "style" attribute in the HTML tag.

```
<p style="color: red; font-size: 18px;">This is an example of inline CSS.</p>
```

Internal CSS: Internal CSS is used to apply styles to a specific HTML document. To use internal CSS, you need to add a "style" tag to the "head" section of your HTML document. You can add multiple CSS styles within the "style" tag.

```
<!DOCTYPE html>
<html>
    <head>
        <title>Internal CSS Example</title>
        <style>
            body {
                background-color: lightblue;
            }

            h1 {
                color: white;
                text-align: center;
            }
        </style>
    </head>
    <body>
        <h1>This is an example of internal CSS</h1>
        <p>Some text</p>
    </body>
</html>
```

External CSS: External CSS is used to apply styles to multiple HTML documents. To use external CSS, you need to create a separate CSS file with the ".css" extension and link it to your HTML document using the "link" tag in the "head" section. You can add multiple CSS styles within the external CSS file.

```html
<!DOCTYPE html>
<html>
  <head>
    <title>External CSS Example</title>
    <link rel="stylesheet" type="text/css" href="style.css">
  </head>
  <body>
    <h1>This is an example of external CSS</h1>
    <p>Some text</p>
  </body>
</html>
```

In the above example, "style.css" is the external CSS file that is linked to the HTML document. You can add CSS styles in the "style.css" file as follows:

```css
body {
  background-color: lightblue;
}

h1 {
  color: white;
  text-align: center;
}
```

In conclusion, CSS is an essential component of web development as it allows developers to add style, layout, and visual effects to their HTML pages. CSS can be added to an HTML page using various methods such as inline, internal, and external stylesheets. Each method has its advantages and disadvantages, and the choice of method depends on the specific needs of the project. Additionally, CSS frameworks and preprocessors like SCSS can also be used to simplify and streamline the CSS development process. By mastering CSS, web developers can create beautiful, engaging, and responsive web pages that are both functional and aesthetically pleasing.

Selectors

In CSS, selectors are used to target and style specific HTML elements. There are several types of selectors that can be used to target elements based on their tag name, class, ID, attributes, and more. Here are some examples of commonly used selectors:

- **Tag Selector:** This selector targets elements based on their tag name. For example, if you want to target all the <p> elements on your page, you can use the following CSS:

- **Class Selector:** This selector targets elements based on their class attribute. For example, if you have a <div> element with the class "container", you can target it with the following CSS:

- **ID Selector:** This selector targets elements based on their ID attribute. IDs are unique on a page, so you can only target one element at a time with an ID selector. For example, if you have a <div> element with the ID "header", you can target it with the following CSS:

```css
#header {
  font-size: 24px;
}
```

- **Attribute Selector:** This selector targets elements based on their attributes. For example, if you have an <input> element with the type "submit", you can target it with the following CSS:

```css
input[type="submit"] {
  background-color: green;
}
```

- **Descendant Selector:** This selector targets elements that are descendants of a particular element. For example, if you have a <div> element with the class "container" and you want to target all the <p> elements inside it, you can use the following CSS:

```css
.container p {
  font-style: italic;
}
```

These are just a few examples of the many selectors that can be used in CSS. Understanding how to use selectors effectively is an important part of writing good CSS.

Box Model

The box model is a fundamental concept in CSS that describes how elements on a web page are structured and sized. It consists of four layers that make up the visual appearance of an element: the content layer, padding layer, border layer, and margin layer.

- The content layer refers to the actual content of the element, such as text, images, or videos.
- The padding layer is the space between the content and the border. It can be used to add extra space within an element, such as adding space around text.
- The border layer is a line that surrounds the padding and content layers. It can be styled to be a solid line, a dashed line, or any other type of line.
- The margin layer is the space between the border of an element and the next element on the page. It can be used to create space between elements and to control the layout of the page.

Here is an example of how the box model works:

```html
<!DOCTYPE html>
<html>
<head>
    <style>
        .box {
            width: 200px;
            height: 100px;
            background-color: blue;
            padding: 20px;
            border: 5px solid black;
            margin: 10px;
        }
    </style>
</head>
<body>
    <div class="box">
        This is an example of the box model.
    </div>
</body>
</html>
```

In this example, we have created a div element with a class of "box". We have applied styles to this element using CSS, including a width of 200 pixels, a height of 100 pixels, a blue background color, 20 pixels of padding, a 5 pixel solid black border, and 10 pixels of margin.

These styles are applied to the box model layers as follows:

- The content layer is 200 pixels wide and 100 pixels high, and contains the text "This is an example of the box model."
- The padding layer is 20 pixels wide on all sides, creating extra space between the content and the border.
- The border layer is a 5 pixel solid black line that surrounds the padding and content layers.
- The margin layer is 10 pixels on all sides, creating space between the border of the box and the next element on the page.

Understanding the box model is crucial for creating layouts in CSS, and knowing how to use the different layers can help you control the spacing and positioning of elements on your web page.

Flex Box

Flexbox is a CSS layout module that makes it easier to design flexible responsive layout structures without having to rely on floats or positioning.

Flexbox works by using a flex container, which is the parent element containing one or more flex items. The container is set to display: flex; to enable flexbox properties.

Here are some key properties that can be used with Flexbox:

- **flex-direction:** defines the direction of the flex container (row, row-reverse, column, or column-reverse).
- **justify-content:** aligns flex items along the main axis (start, end, center, space-between, or space-around).
- **align-items:** aligns flex items along the cross axis (start, end, center, baseline, or stretch).
- **flex-wrap:** specifies if flex items should wrap to multiple lines or not (wrap, nowrap, or wrap-reverse).
- **flex-grow:** specifies how much the flex item should grow relative to the other flex items.
- **flex-shrink:** specifies how much the flex item should shrink relative to the other flex items.

- **flex-basis:** specifies the initial size of the flex item before any available space is distributed.
- **order:** specifies the order of the flex item within the flex container.

Here is an example showing the flex box:

```html
<div class="container">
  <div class="box box-1">Box 1</div>
  <div class="box box-2">Box 2</div>
  <div class="box box-3">Box 3</div>
</div>
```

```css
.container {
  display: flex;
  flex-direction: row;
  justify-content: space-between;
  align-items: center;
  flex-wrap: wrap;
}

.box {
  flex-grow: 1;
  flex-shrink: 1;
  flex-basis: 30%;
  height: 200px;
  background-color: #f2f2f2;
  border: 1px solid #ccc;
  box-sizing: border-box;
}

@media screen and (max-width: 768px) {
  .box {
    flex-basis: 100%;
  }
}
```

In this example, the container element has been set to display as a flex container with a row direction. The boxes inside the container have been given flex properties to enable them to resize and shift depending on the size of the container. The justify-content property is set to space-between to create equal spacing between the boxes. The flex-wrap property is set to wrap to allow the boxes to wrap onto multiple lines. Finally, a media query has been added to change the flex-basis property of the boxes when the screen size is smaller than 768px to make them stack vertically.

Media Query & Responsive Design

With the rise of mobile devices and varying screen sizes, creating responsive designs has become crucial. Media queries are the cornerstone of responsive design. They allow developers to create different styles for different device sizes and orientations.

Media queries allow developers to apply CSS rules based on the device's characteristics, such as screen size, resolution, and orientation. The @media rule is used to define different styles for different media types and devices.

```css
/* Default styles for all devices */
body {
    font-size: 16px;
    background-color: #f8f8f8;
}

/* Styles for devices with a max-width of 768px */
@media screen and (max-width: 768px) {
    body {
        font-size: 14px;
    }
    .container {
        width: 90%;
    }
}

/* Styles for devices with a max-width of 480px */
@media screen and (max-width: 480px) {
    body {
        font-size: 12px;
    }
    .container {
        width: 100%;
    }
}
```

Media queries and responsive design are crucial aspects of modern web design. They allow developers to create a seamless experience for users across all devices and screen sizes. With these tools, developers can ensure that their web pages are accessible and optimized for all users, regardless of the device they are using.

Grid

CSS Grid is a layout system in CSS that allows designers to create complex grid layouts for their websites. It is a 2-dimensional system that uses rows and columns to arrange elements on a web page. CSS Grid is very flexible and can be used to create a wide range of layouts, from simple to complex.

Here's an example of a basic grid layout with two columns and two rows:

```html
<div class="container">
    <div class="box1">Box 1</div>
    <div class="box2">Box 2</div>
    <div class="box3">Box 3</div>
    <div class="box4">Box 4</div>
</div>

<style>
    .container {
        display: grid;
        grid-template-columns: 1fr 1fr;
        grid-template-rows: 1fr 1fr;
        gap: 20px;
    }

    .box1 {
        background-color: #4CAF50;
        color: white;
        padding: 20px;
    }

    .box2 {
        background-color: #2196F3;
        color: white;
        padding: 20px;
    }

    .box3 {
        background-color: #f44336;
        color: white;
        padding: 20px;
    }

    .box4 {
        background-color: #FFC107;
        color: white;
        padding: 20px;
    }
</style>
```

To use CSS Grid, you need to define a container element as a grid using the display property with the value "grid". Then, you can define rows and columns using the grid-template-rows and grid-template-columns properties.

In this example, we define a container element with the class "container". We set the display property to "grid" to create a grid layout. We define two rows and two columns using the grid-template-rows and grid-template-columns properties. We also set a gap of 20 pixels between the grid items using the gap property.

Then, we define four grid items with the classes "box1", "box2", "box3", and "box4". We set their background colors, text colors, and padding to make them stand out.

CSS Grid is a powerful tool for creating complex layouts in CSS. It allows designers to create responsive and flexible layouts that can adapt to different screen sizes and devices. With CSS Grid, you can create beautiful and functional designs without relying on external libraries or frameworks.

When working with CSS Grid, there are some common mistakes that beginners might make. One of the most common mistakes is not defining the grid container properly. It is important to define the grid container with the display: grid; property, otherwise, the grid layout will not work.

Another mistake is not setting the appropriate column and row sizes, which can cause the grid to appear distorted or not display properly. It is also important to consider the responsiveness of the grid and to use appropriate media queries to adjust the grid layout for different screen sizes.

With a good understanding of these concepts and attention to detail, you can effectively use CSS Grid to create beautiful and responsive layouts for your web pages.

Pseudo Elements & Classes

Pseudo-elements and pseudo-classes are powerful features of CSS that allow developers to style specific parts of an HTML document based on their attributes or position in the document.

Pseudo-elements are used to style specific parts of an element, such as the first letter or line of a paragraph.

They are represented by two colons (::) and are used with an element selector. Here is an example of using the ::first-letter pseudo-element to style the first letter of a paragraph:

```css
p::first-letter {
    font-size: 2em;
    color: red;
}
```

This will apply the styles to the first letter of every paragraph element in the HTML document.

List of available elements

- ::before
- ::after
- ::first-letter
- ::first-line
- ::selection

Pseudo-classes, on the other hand, are used to style elements based on their attributes or state, such as when a link is being hovered over or clicked. Pseudo-classes are represented by a single colon (:), and are used with a class or ID selector.

Here is an example of using the :hover pseudo-class to style a link when it is being hovered over:

```css
a:hover {
    color: blue;
    text-decoration: underline;
}
```

Ctrl + Shift + Frontend

This will apply the styles to the link element when the mouse cursor is hovering over it.

Overall, pseudo-elements and pseudo-classes are useful tools in CSS for targeting and styling specific parts of an HTML document based on various conditions.

List of available pseudo classes:

- :hover
- :active
- :focus
- :visited
- :nth-child
- :first-child
- :last-child
- :only-child
- :checked
- :not

Note that pseudo-elements use two colons (::) instead of one colon (:), although both syntaxes are usually supported by modern browsers.

Alignment, Colors & Opacity

```html
<!DOCTYPE html>
<html>
  <head>
    <style>
      /* Define styles for the div element */
      div {
        border: 2px solid #333; /* Add a 2px solid black border */
        color: #fff; /* Set the text color to white */
        background-color: #333; /* Set the background color to black */
        padding: 20px; /* Add 20 pixels of padding to the div element */
        margin: 20px; /* Add 20 pixels of margin to the div element */
        text-align: center; /* Center the text in the div element */
        opacity: 0.8; /* Set the opacity of the div element to 80% */
      }
    </style>
  </head>
  <body>
    <div>
      <h1>Hello, World!</h1>
      <p>This is an example of using borders, colors, padding, margin, alignment, backgrounds, and opacity in CSS.</p>
    </div>
  </body>
</html>
```

In this example, we've defined a style rule for a div element that sets several different properties.

The border property adds a 2 pixel solid black border around the div. The color property sets the text color to white, while the background-color property sets the background color to black.

The padding property adds 20 pixels of space inside the div element, while the margin property adds 20 pixels of space outside the div element.

The text-align property centers the text inside the div element, and the opacity property sets the opacity of the element to 80%.

These properties can be adjusted to create different effects, and they are often used in combination to create visually appealing layouts and designs.

Z-index

Z-index is a CSS property that is used to control the positioning of elements on top of each other in the z-axis. It is commonly used in conjunction with the position property to create a layered effect on a webpage. The z-index property specifies the stack order of an element. An element with a higher z-index value will appear above an element with a lower z-index value. If two elements have the same z-index value, the element that appears last in the HTML code will appear on top.

```html
<!DOCTYPE html>
<html>
<head>
    <title>Z-index Example</title>
    <style>
        #element1 {
            background-color: red;
            position: absolute;
            top: 20px;
            left: 20px;
            width: 200px;
            height: 200px;
            z-index: 1;
        }

        #element2 {
            background-color: blue;
            position: absolute;
            top: 50px;
            left: 50px;
            width: 200px;
            height: 200px;
            z-index: 2;
        }

        #element3 {
            background-color: green;
            position: absolute;
            top: 80px;
            left: 80px;
            width: 200px;
            height: 200px;
            z-index: 3;
        }
    </style>
</head>
<body>
    <div id="element1">Element 1</div>
    <div id="element2">Element 2</div>
    <div id="element3">Element 3</div>
</body>
</html>
```

In this example, we have three elements, each with a different z-index value. The first element has a z-index of 1, the second element has a z-index of 2, and the third element has a z-index of 3.

This means that the third element will appear on top of the other two elements, the second element will appear on top of the first element, and the first element will appear at the bottom.

It is important to note that z-index only works on elements that have a position property of either absolute, relative, or fixed. Additionally, it is best to use z-index sparingly and only when necessary, as using too many layers can make the page harder to manage and slow down the website's performance.

One common use case for z-index is to control the stacking order of overlapping elements. For example, if you have a navigation bar and a slideshow on your website, you might want to make sure the navigation bar appears on top of the slideshow so that users can still access it. You can accomplish this by giving the navigation bar a higher z-index value than the slideshow.

It's important to be careful with z-index, however, as setting a very high value can cause elements to overlap in unintended ways. In addition, using z-index on too many elements can make it difficult to manage the stacking order of your elements. It's always a good idea to use z-index sparingly and with intention.

```css
#navigation {
    position: fixed;
    z-index: 1000;
}

#slideshow {
    position: relative;
    z-index: 500;
}
```

In this example, the #navigation element has a higher z-index value than the #slideshow element, which ensures that the navigation bar appears on top of the slideshow.

Animations & Transitions

Animations and transitions are a powerful tool in CSS that allow you to create dynamic and engaging user interfaces.

Animations allow you to create motion in your webpage while transitions allow you to add smooth and gradual changes between two states of an element.

CSS animations are created using the @keyframes rule, which allows you to specify multiple styles for an element at different keyframes or points in time.

You can then use the animation property to apply the animation to an element and control its duration, timing function, and delay.

```css
.square {
    width: 50px;
    height: 50px;
    background-color: red;
    animation-name: rotate;
    animation-duration: 2s;
    animation-timing-function: linear;
    animation-iteration-count: infinite;
}

@keyframes rotate {
    0% {
        transform: rotate(0deg);
    }
    100% {
        transform: rotate(360deg);
    }
}
```

In this example, we've created a @keyframes rule named rotate that defines the rotation of the square element. We've then applied this animation to the .square class using the animation property, specifying its duration, timing function, and iteration count.

CSS transitions, on the other hand, are created using the transition property, which allows you to define a gradual transition between two states of an element.

You can specify the property to transition, the duration of the transition, and the timing function that controls the speed of the transition.

```css
button {
  background-color: blue;
  color: white;
  transition: background-color 0.5s ease;
}

button:hover {
  background-color: red;
}
```

In this example, we've defined a transition for the background-color property of the button element, specifying its duration and timing function.

When the button is hovered over, the background color changes smoothly from blue to red over the specified duration.

- animation-delay
- animation-direction
- animation-duration
- animation-fill-mode
- animation-iteration-count
- animation-name
- animation-play-state
- animation-timing-function
- transition-delay
- transition-duration
- transition-property
- transition-timing-function

These properties can be used to fine-tune and customize the animations and transitions in CSS to achieve the desired effects.

Ctrl + Shift + Frontend

Chapter 2 Project

For this chapter's project, we want you to take your personal website from chapter 1 and decorate it with CSS. Add some color, adjust the font, and make your website eye-catching and beautiful. Remember, the goal of this project is to have fun and let your creativity run wild!

Here are some guidelines to help you get started:

- Use CSS to add some color to your website. Experiment with different color palettes to find the one that suits your personality the best.
- Play around with different fonts and font sizes. Use CSS to adjust the font of your headers, paragraphs, and other text elements.
- Add some images and adjust their position and size using CSS. Try to make your images blend well with your website's color scheme.
- Experiment with padding and margins to adjust the spacing between your elements. Use CSS to align your elements to the left, right, center, or justify them.
- Add some background images or colors to your website to give it more depth and personality.
- Try using animations and transitions to add some movement and interactivity to your website.

Remember, this project is all about having fun and expressing yourself through code. Don't be afraid to experiment and try new things. Let your imagination guide you and have fun along the way!

We can't wait to see what you come up with. Happy coding!

CHAPTER 3

Version Control and CSS Framework

Welcome to chapter 3! In this chapter, we'll be exploring two important topics in web development - version control system and CSS framework.

Version control system is an essential tool for developers to keep track of changes made to code over time. It allows multiple developers to collaborate on a project while keeping track of their changes and ensuring a smooth workflow.

CSS frameworks, on the other hand, are pre-designed CSS styles that can be easily applied to your HTML code to give your website a polished and professional look. They can save you a lot of time and effort when designing a website, as they already provide a pre-built structure and styling for your website.

We'll be diving into these topics in more detail in the upcoming lessons, so get ready to level up your web development skills!

Version Control

This chapter, we're going to talk about an essential tool for any developer: version control. Don't worry, it's not as scary as it sounds!

Version control is the practice of managing changes to your code over time. It allows you to keep track of what changes you've made, who made them, and when. This is crucial for collaboration, troubleshooting, and ensuring the stability and consistency of your codebase.

For this chapter, we'll be using Git as our version control system. Git is a popular and powerful tool that enables you to keep track of your changes, branch your work, collaborate with others, and more.

But we won't stop there! We'll also be exploring GitHub, a web-based platform for hosting, sharing, and collaborating on Git repositories. It's a fantastic tool for working on projects with a team, contributing to open-source projects, and showcasing your work to the world.

Ctrl + Shift + Frontend

So get ready to learn the basics of version control with Git and explore the powerful features of GitHub. It's time to take control of your code and take your development skills to the next level!

Git

Git is a distributed version control system that helps developers track changes in their code and collaborate with others. It allows for efficient code management and organization, and also provides the ability to easily roll back to previous versions of the code. Git is an essential tool for any software development project, and its popularity and widespread adoption have made it the go-to choice for version control in the industry. So get ready to dive into the world of Git and start managing your code like a pro!

Installation

Download Git:

- Go to the official Git website.
- Choose the appropriate download for your operating system and download the installer.

Install Git:

- Once the download is complete, run the installer and follow the prompts.
- On the "Select Components" screen, leave the default settings unless you have a specific need for something else.
- On the "Choosing the default editor used by Git" screen, select your preferred text editor (if applicable).
- On the "Configuring the line ending conversions" screen, leave the default settings unless you have a specific need for something else.
- On the "Configuring extra options" screen, leave the default settings unless you have a specific need for something else.
- On the "Choosing the HTTPS transport backend" screen, leave the default settings unless you have a specific need for something else.
- On the "Configuring experimental performance tweaks" screen, leave the default settings unless you have a specific need for something else.
- On the "Completing the Git Setup Wizard" screen, click "Finish".

Open a command prompt:

- On Windows, open the "Command Prompt" or "Git Bash" application.
- On Mac or Linux, open the terminal application.

Set your username:

Type the following command, replacing "Your Name" with your actual name:

```
git config --global user.name "Your Name"
```

Set your email address:

Type the following command, replacing "youremail@example.com" with your actual email address:

```
git config --global user.email "youremail@example.com"
```

Great, now we have set up git on your device, let's try to use it to track our files.

Usage of Git

Basic Commands :

- **git init:** This command initializes a new Git repository in your current directory. It's like telling Git, "Hey, keep an eye on this folder and its contents from now on!"
- **git add:** This command adds changes you've made to files in your working directory to the staging area. It's like telling Git, "Hey, these changes are important and I want to include them in my next commit!"

Ctrl + Shift + Frontend

- **git commit:** This command creates a snapshot of the changes in the staging area and saves it to the repository. It's like telling Git, "Hey, remember this exact moment in time, when these changes were made and what they were!"
- **git status:** Shows the status of files in the repository, including whether they are untracked, modified, or staged.
- **git log:** Displays a log of all the commits made to the repository, including the commit message, author, and date.

Here are some code snippets showing how to use Git with a folder containing an HTML and CSS file:

Initialize Git in the folder:

```
cd /path/to/folder
git init
```

Add the files to the staging area:

```
git add index.html style.css
```

Commit the changes with a message:

```
git commit -m "Added index.html and style.css"
```

Ctrl + Shift + Frontend

Check the status of the repository:

View the commit history:

Note that these commands assume that Git is already installed on your computer and that you are working in a terminal or command prompt. Also, it's a good practice to add a **.gitignore** file to your repository to exclude any files or folders that you don't want to track with Git.

Github

- Create a GitHub account (if you don't already have one) by going to GitHub and following the sign-up process.
- Once you're logged in to GitHub, click on the "+" icon in the top right corner of the screen and select "New repository" from the dropdown menu.
- Give your new repository a name and a brief description, and make sure the repository is set to "Public" (unless you want to keep it private).
- Check the box that says "Initialize this repository with a README" (this will create a basic README file in your repository).
- Click on the "Create repository" button to create your new repository.
- Link your local repository to the remote repository using the following command:

```
git remote add origin <remote repository URL>
```

- Push your code to the remote repository using the following command:

```
git push -u origin master
```

Congratulations, you've successfully pushed your code to GitHub! You can now proudly share your project with others, and have a secure backup of your work. Keep up the great work, and remember to continue using version control and GitHub to make your development process smoother and more efficient. Happy coding! 🎉

Css Framework

CSS Frameworks are pre-written libraries of CSS code that help developers build websites and web applications more quickly and easily. Instead of writing all of the CSS code from scratch, developers can use a framework to apply pre-designed styles to their HTML code.

In this, we'll be introducing you to two popular CSS frameworks: Tailwind CSS and Bootstrap. Both of these frameworks offer a variety of pre-built CSS classes that you can apply to your HTML code to create responsive, modern designs.

CSS Frameworks are pre-written CSS code that makes it easier for you to create visually appealing websites without having to start from scratch every time. And guess what? You have a choice between two popular frameworks - Tailwind CSS and Bootstrap. Yes, we are giving you the freedom to choose whichever you like better and use it throughout the projects. However, choosing both is not the right way to go about it, so pick the one you fancy the most, and let's dive right in!

Bootstrap

Bootstrap is a popular CSS framework that allows developers to create responsive and mobile-first websites with ease. It provides a collection of pre-built HTML, CSS, and JavaScript components that can be used to build a variety of web pages and user interfaces.

Bootstrap has a wide range of features, including a grid system, responsive design, and extensive documentation. It is also highly customizable and can be used to create both simple and complex designs.

Getting Started

Step 1: Download Bootstrap

The first step is to download Bootstrap from the official website. You can download the precompiled files or use a package manager like npm.

Step 2: Include Bootstrap in Your HTML

Once you have downloaded Bootstrap, you need to include it in your HTML file. You can either link to the CSS and JavaScript files or use a CDN. Here's an example of how to include Bootstrap using a CDN:

```html
<!-- CSS -->
<link rel="stylesheet" href="https://maxcdn.bootstrapcdn.com/bootstrap/4.5.2/css/bootstrap.min.css">

<!-- JavaScript -->
<script src="https://ajax.googleapis.com/ajax/libs/jquery/3.5.1/jquery.min.js"></script>
<script src="https://cdnjs.cloudflare.com/ajax/libs/popper.js/1.16.0/umd/popper.min.js"></script>
<script src="https://maxcdn.bootstrapcdn.com/bootstrap/4.5.2/js/bootstrap.min.js"></script>
```

Step 3: Start Using Bootstrap

Once you have included Bootstrap in your HTML file, you can start using its classes and components to create your website. Here's an example of how to create a simple Bootstrap navbar:

```html
<nav class="navbar navbar-expand-lg navbar-light bg-light">
    <a class="navbar-brand" href="#">My Website</a>
    <button class="navbar-toggler" type="button" data-toggle="collapse" data-target="#navbarNav" aria-controls="navbarNav" aria-expanded="false" aria-label="Toggle navigation">
        <span class="navbar-toggler-icon"></span>
    </button>
    <div class="collapse navbar-collapse" id="navbarNav">
        <ul class="navbar-nav">
            <li class="nav-item active">
                <a class="nav-link" href="#">Home</a>
            </li>
            <li class="nav-item">
                <a class="nav-link" href="#">About</a>
            </li>
            <li class="nav-item">
                <a class="nav-link" href="#">Contact</a>
            </li>
        </ul>
    </div>
</nav>
```

In this example, we have used the navbar class to create a navbar, the navbar-brand class to create a logo or brand name, the navbar-toggler class to create a toggle button for mobile devices, and the navbar-nav class to create a list of navigation links.

These are just a few examples of how to use Bootstrap. The framework comes with many other classes and components that you can use to create a variety of website designs, feel free to explore the documentation and references.

Ctrl + Shift + Frontend

Tailwind CSS

(If your choice is Bootstrap you can skip this section)

Tailwind CSS is a utility-first CSS framework that makes it easy to create custom designs without having to write any CSS from scratch. It provides pre-defined CSS classes that can be used to quickly style your HTML elements.

To use Tailwind CSS in your project, you can either download and include the pre-built CSS file or install it as a dependency in your project using a package manager like npm.

Once you have included or installed Tailwind CSS, you can start using its classes to style your HTML elements. For example, you can add the "text-center" class to a heading element to center its text, or the "bg-blue-500" class to a div element to give it a blue background color.

Getting Started

To get started, you first need to install Tailwind CSS by following these steps:

Open your command line interface (CLI) and navigate to the project directory where you want to use Tailwind CSS.

npm (short for Node Package Manager) is a package manager for the JavaScript programming language. It helps developers install, share, and manage dependencies or packages for their projects.

To download npm, you can visit their official website. From there, you can choose the appropriate installation method based on your operating system.

Once node and npm is installed on your machine, you can use it to install packages and dependencies for your projects, including Tailwind CSS.

Run the following command to install Tailwind CSS using npm:

Ctrl + Shift + Frontend

```
npm install tailwindcss
```

Once installed, you can create a new file named tailwind.css in your project directory and add the following code:

```
@tailwind base;
@tailwind components;
@tailwind utilities;
```

Next, you need to include the tailwind.css file in your HTML file by adding the following code in the <head> section:

```
<link rel="stylesheet" href="./tailwind.css">
```

Finally, you can start using Tailwind CSS classes in your HTML and CSS files to style your elements. For example, you can use the following code to add a blue background color to a <div> element:

```
<div class="bg-blue-500">This div has a blue background color</div>
```

In this example, bg-blue-500 is a Tailwind CSS class that adds a blue background color to the element. That's it! You're now ready to start using Tailwind CSS in your project. With Tailwind CSS, you can easily customize your styles by combining different utility classes to create your own unique design. Have fun exploring!

```
<!DOCTYPE html>
<html lang="en">
<head>
    <meta charset="UTF-8">
    <meta name="viewport" content="width=device-width, initial-scale=1.0">
    <title>Tailwind Example</title>
    <link rel="stylesheet" href="https://cdn.jsdelivr.net/npm/tailwindcss@latest/dist/tailwind.min.css">
</head>
<body>
    <div class="bg-blue-500 p-6">
        <h1 class="text-white text-3xl">Welcome to my website!</h1>
        <p class="text-white text-lg mt-4">This is an example of how to use Tailwind CSS in your HTML.</p>
    </div>
</body>
</html>
```

With this we come to the end of chapter 3, let's dive into the project section

Chapter 3 Project

Project: Create a Recipe Website

Instructions:

- Choose a cuisine that you are passionate about or interested in, and create a website that showcases recipes from that cuisine.

- Design your website layout using either Bootstrap or Tailwind CSS. Use components such as navbar, grid system, and cards to create a visually appealing and responsive design.

- Create a homepage that welcomes the user to your website and gives an overview of the cuisine you have chosen. Include a search bar, a featured recipe section, and links to different categories of recipes.

- Create category pages that list different types of recipes such as appetizers, entrees, desserts, etc. Each category page should include a grid of recipe cards.

- Create individual recipe pages that display the recipe name, a picture of the dish, a list of ingredients, and the recipe instructions.

- Add a "submit a recipe" form that allows users to submit their own recipes to your website.

- Use CSS to add hover effects, animations, and other design elements that make your website look polished and professional.

- Push your code to a GitHub repository and host your website on a free hosting platform like GitHub Pages.

Remember to have fun with this project and be creative with your design and content! Good luck!

CHAPTER 4

This chapter, you'll learn the fundamentals of JavaScript and explore how to use it to add interactive features to your web pages. You'll start by learning the basics of the language, including variables, data types, and control flow. From there, you'll move on to more advanced topics like functions, objects, and events.

JavaScript is a versatile programming language that can be used in various contexts, such as web development, mobile app development, game development, desktop application development, and more. Some specific use cases of JavaScript include:

- Building interactive and dynamic web pages with features like form validation, DOM manipulation, animations, and user interface enhancements.
- Creating server-side applications with frameworks like Node.js that allow developers to use JavaScript on the backend as well.
- Developing cross-platform mobile applications using frameworks like React Native or Ionic.
- Designing desktop applications with the help of tools like Electron, which allows developers to use web technologies like HTML, CSS, and JavaScript to build desktop applications that work across multiple operating systems.
- Creating interactive games and animations with HTML5 canvas and other game engines that use JavaScript.

JavaScript is a popular and widely used language, making it a valuable skill for developers in various industries.

Getting Started

To get started with JavaScript, you can either embed your code directly into an HTML document using a <script> tag, or you can create a separate JavaScript file and link to it from your HTML document using a <script> tag with a src attribute.

Here's an example of embedding JavaScript directly into an HTML document:

Ctrl + Shift + Frontend

```html
<!DOCTYPE html>
<html>
<head>
    <title>Hello World</title>
</head>
<body>

    <h1>Hello World!</h1>

    <script>
        alert('Hello World!');
    </script>

</body>
</html>
```

In this example, we have an HTML document with an H1 heading that says "Hello World!" and a JavaScript block that displays an alert dialog box with the same message.

You can also run JavaScript code in the browser console. To access the console, simply open the developer tools in your browser (usually by pressing F12 or Ctrl+Shift+I) and switch to the "Console" tab. You can then type JavaScript commands directly into the console and see their output.

Here's an example of running "Hello World!" in the browser console:

```
console.log('Hello World!');
```

To run JS using node js follow the below steps :

- Install Node.js by going to the official website and downloading the installer for your operating system. Follow the installation instructions to complete the setup process.
- Open a text editor and create a new file named "hello.js".
- Add the following code to the file:

```
console.log('Hello World!');
```

- Save the file.
- Open a command prompt or terminal window.
- Navigate to the directory where the "hello.js" file is saved.

```
node hello.js
```

To embed JavaScript code into an HTML file from an external file, you can use the following steps:

- Create a separate JavaScript file with the .js extension and save it with a meaningful name. For example, script.js.
- In the HTML file where you want to use the JavaScript code, include the following code inside the <head> section:

```
<head>
    <script src="path/to/script.js"></script>
</head>
```

Replace path/to/script.js with the actual path to your JavaScript file.

- Write your JavaScript code inside the external JavaScript file (script.js in this example).

Ctrl + Shift + Frontend

- Open the HTML file in a web browser, and open the developer console. You should see the "Hello, world!" message displayed in the console.
- If you're using Google Chrome, you can open the developer console by pressing Ctrl + Shift + J (Windows/Linux) or Cmd + Option + J (Mac).
- The external JavaScript file will be loaded and executed automatically when the HTML file is loaded in the browser.

These are the various ways in which you can run javascript. Now let's dive into the language.

Variable and Data Types

In JavaScript, variables are used to store data values. A variable can be declared using the var, let, or const keyword followed by the variable name.

In this example, the variable greeting is declared and assigned the value "Hello World!". The var keyword is used to declare the variable.

JavaScript has several built-in data types, including:

- **Strings**: Used to represent text data, and are enclosed in single or double quotes.

60

- **Numbers**: Used to represent numeric data, including integers and floating point numbers.
- **Booleans**: Used to represent true/false values.
- **Null**: Used to represent a deliberate non-value.
- **Undefined**: Used to represent a variable that has been declared but not yet assigned a value.
- **Objects**: Used to represent complex data structures, including arrays and functions.

Here is an example of declaring variables of different data types:

```javascript
var name = "John";
var age = 30;
var isStudent = true;
var car = null;
var job;
var hobbies = ["reading", "cooking", "traveling"];
```

In this example, we have declared variables name, age, isStudent, car, job, and hobbies, each with a different data type.

It's important to note that var is function-scoped, whereas let and const are block-scoped. In general, it is recommended to use let and const instead of var for declaring variables.

Conditional Statements and Loops

Conditional statements and loops are essential building blocks in programming. In JavaScript, there are several types of conditional statements and loops available to use.

Conditional Statements :

Conditional statements allow you to execute different code depending on whether a condition is true or false. The most common conditional statement in JavaScript is the if statement:

```js
let num = 10;

if (num > 5) {
  console.log("Number is greater than 5");
} else {
  console.log("Number is less than or equal to 5");
}
```

In this example, if num is greater than 5, the code inside the if block will be executed, otherwise, the code inside the else block will be executed.

Another useful conditional statement is the switch statement, which allows you to test a variable against multiple values:

```js
let day = "Monday";

switch (day) {
  case "Monday":
    console.log("Today is Monday");
    break;
  case "Tuesday":
    console.log("Today is Tuesday");
    break;
  default:
    console.log("Today is another day");
}
```

In this example, the value of day is tested against multiple cases using the switch statement. If the value matches a case, the corresponding code block will be executed. If no matches are found, the default code block will be executed.

Loops:

Loops allow you to execute a block of code multiple times. The two most common types of loops in JavaScript are the for loop and the while loop.

The for loop is used when you know how many times you need to loop:

```
for (let i = 0; i < 5; i++) {
    console.log(i);
}
```

In this example, the loop will execute 5 times, with i starting at 0 and incrementing by 1 on each iteration.

The while loop is used when you don't know how many times you need to loop:

```
let i = 0;
while (i < 5) {
    console.log(i);
    i++;
}
```

In this example, the loop will continue executing as long as i is less than 5, with i incrementing by 1 on each iteration.

Overall, conditional statements and loops are essential tools for any JavaScript programmer. With these constructs, you can build complex programs that respond to different conditions and iterate over data sets.

Functions

Functions are a fundamental building block in JavaScript. They allow you to encapsulate a piece of code and call it from anywhere in your program. Functions are defined using the function keyword, followed by the name of the function, and then a pair of parentheses that can contain zero or more parameters. The body of the function is enclosed in curly braces { }.

Here is an example of a simple function that takes two parameters and returns their sum:

```js
function add(a, b) {
    return a + b;
}
```

In the example above, we defined a function called add that takes two parameters a and b. Inside the function, we used the return keyword to specify the value that the function should return. In this case, the function returns the sum of a and b.

Once you have defined a function, you can call it from anywhere in your program using its name followed by a pair of parentheses. Here is an example of calling the add function from another part of your program:

```js
let result = add(2, 3);
console.log(result); // Output: 5
```

In the example above, we called the add function and passed it two arguments: 2 and 3. The function returned the sum of these two values (5), which we then assigned to the variable result. We then printed the value of the result to the console using the console.log() function.

Functions can also be used to perform more complex tasks. For example, you might write a function that takes an array of numbers as input, sorts the numbers in ascending order, and then returns the sorted array. Here is an example of such a function:

```
function sortNumbers(numbers) {
  numbers.sort(function(a, b) {
    return a - b;
  });
  return numbers;
}
```

In the example above, we defined a function called sortNumbers that takes an array of numbers as input. Inside the function, we used the sort() method to sort the numbers in ascending order. We passed a comparison function to the sort() method to tell it how to compare the numbers. Finally, we returned the sorted array from the function.

Once you have defined a function, you can call it from anywhere in your program just like any other function. Here is an example of calling the sortNumbers function:

```
let numbers = [3, 1, 4, 1, 5, 9, 2, 6, 5, 3, 5];
let sortedNumbers = sortNumbers(numbers);
console.log(sortedNumbers); // Output: [1, 1, 2, 3, 3, 4, 5, 5, 5, 6, 9]
```

In the example above, we called the sortNumbers function and passed it an array of numbers. The function sorted the numbers and returned the sorted array, which we then assigned to the variable sortedNumbers. We then printed the value of sortedNumbers to the console using the console.log() function.

Inbuilt Functions

Here are some commonly used built-in methods in JavaScript that are useful for front-end development:

- **getElementById():** This method is used to get an HTML element by its ID. It returns the element as an object, which can then be manipulated using JavaScript.

- **querySelector():** This method is used to select the first element that matches a specified CSS selector. It returns the element as an object, which can then be manipulated using JavaScript.
- **addEventListener():** This method is used to attach an event listener to an HTML element. It takes two parameters: the type of event to listen for (such as "click" or "mouseover"), and the function to be executed when the event occurs.
- **classList.add():** This method is used to add a CSS class to an HTML element. It takes one parameter: the name of the class to be added.
- **classList.remove():** This method is used to remove a CSS class from an HTML element. It takes one parameter: the name of the class to be removed.
- **setAttribute():** This method is used to set the value of a specified attribute on an HTML element. It takes two parameters: the name of the attribute, and the value to be set.
- **getAttribute():** This method is used to get the value of a specified attribute on an HTML element. It takes one parameter: the name of the attribute.
- **innerHTML:** This property is used to get or set the HTML content of an element. It can be used to dynamically change the contents of an element based on user input or other events.
- **style:** This property is used to get or set the CSS styling of an element. It can be used to dynamically change the appearance of an element based on user input or other events.

```javascript
const myElement = document.getElementById("myId");
const myElement = document.querySelector(".myClass");
myElement.addEventListener("click", myFunction);
myElement.classList.add("myClass");
myElement.classList.remove("myClass");
myElement.setAttribute("src", "myImage.jpg");
const mySrc = myElement.getAttribute("src");
myElement.innerHTML = "New content";
myElement.style.backgroundColor = "red";
```

The map() function in JavaScript is used to create a new array by transforming each element of an existing array. It applies a given function to each element of the array and returns a new array with the transformed elements.

Here is an example of how to use map():

```js
const arr = [1, 2, 3, 4];
const newArr = arr.map((num) => num * 2);
console.log(newArr); // Output: [2, 4, 6, 8]
```

In this example, we first create an array arr with 4 elements. We then apply the map() function to it, which transforms each element of the arr array by multiplying it with 2. The transformed elements are then stored in a new array newArr. Finally, we log the newArr array to the console.

The filter() function in JavaScript is used to create a new array by filtering out elements that do not meet a certain condition. It applies a given function to each element of the array and returns a new array with only the elements that meet the condition.

Here is an example of how to use filter():

```js
const arr = [1, 2, 3, 4];
const newArr = arr.filter((num) => num % 2 === 0);
console.log(newArr); // Output: [2, 4]
```

In this example, we first create an array arr with 4 elements. We then apply the filter() function to it, which filters out all the elements that are not even. The filtered elements are then stored in a new array newArr. Finally, we log the newArr array to the console.

Some of the other commonly used functions are as follows :

- **indexOf():** Returns the index of the first occurrence of a specified value in a string or array.
- **split():** Splits a string into an array of substrings based on a specified separator.
- **join():** Joins all elements of an array into a string.

- **push():** Adds one or more elements to the end of an array and returns the new length of the array.
- **pop():** Removes the last element from an array and returns that element.
- **shift():** Removes the first element from an array and returns that element.
- **unshift():** Adds one or more elements to the beginning of an array and returns the new length of the array.
- **slice():** Returns a portion of an array into a new array.
- **splice():** Adds or removes elements from an array.
- **concat():** Joins two or more arrays and returns a new array.

These are just a few examples of commonly used inbuilt functions in JavaScript. There are many more that can be explored and utilized.

Types of Functions

In JavaScript, there are various types of functions, including regular functions, arrow functions, and anonymous functions.

Regular functions:

A regular function is a traditional function that is defined using the function keyword followed by a name and a set of parentheses, which can optionally contain parameters. The body of the function is enclosed in curly braces.

Example:

```javascript
function greet(name) {
  console.log(`Hello, ${name}!`);
}

greet("John"); // Output: "Hello, John!"
```

Arrow functions:

An arrow function is a shorthand way of writing a function that was introduced in ECMAScript 6. Instead of using the function keyword, an arrow function uses an arrow (=>) to indicate the function's definition.

Example:

```javascript
const greet = (name) => {
  console.log(`Hello, ${name}!`);
}

greet("John"); // Output: "Hello, John!"
```

Arrow functions have a more concise syntax and behave differently in certain situations, such as when it comes to this keyword.

Anonymous functions:

An anonymous function is a function that does not have a name. Anonymous functions are often used as callbacks in event listeners and other situations where a function is only used once and does not need to be defined with a name.

Example:

```javascript
document.addEventListener("click", function() {
  console.log("You clicked the document!");
});
```

In addition to these types of functions, JavaScript also supports higher-order functions, which are functions that take other functions as arguments or return functions as values.

These can be useful for tasks such as composing functions and handling asynchronous code.

Callback Functions & Promises

In JavaScript, a callback function is a function that is passed as an argument to another function and is executed inside that function. Callback functions are used to control the order of execution of functions that depend on the result of other functions.

They are commonly used in asynchronous programming, where a function needs to wait for another function to complete before continuing execution.

Here's an example of a simple callback function:

```javascript
function greet(name, callback) {
    console.log(`Hello, ${name}!`);
    callback();
}

function sayGoodbye() {
    console.log('Goodbye!');
}

greet('John', sayGoodbye);
```

In this example, the greet function takes two arguments: a name string and a callback function. The greet function logs a greeting message to the console, then calls the callback function.

The sayGoodbye function is defined separately, and is passed as the callback argument when calling greet.

When greet is executed, it logs the greeting message, then calls the sayGoodbye function, which logs a farewell message to the console.

Promises are another way to control the flow of execution in JavaScript.

A promise represents a value that may not be available yet, but will be resolved at some point in the future. A promise can have three states: pending, fulfilled, or rejected.

Here's an example of a simple promise:

```js
function getData() {
  return new Promise((resolve, reject) => {
    fetch('https://example.com/data')
      .then(response => response.json())
      .then(data => resolve(data))
      .catch(error => reject(error));
  });
}

getData()
  .then(data => console.log(data))
  .catch(error => console.error(error));
```

In this example, the getData function returns a new promise that wraps a call to the fetch function.

When the fetch function resolves with a response, the response is converted to JSON using the json method, and the resulting data is passed to the resolve function of the promise.

If an error occurs during the fetch, it is caught using the catch method and passed to the reject function of the promise.

Finally, the getData function is called, and two methods are chained to the promise it returns: then and catch.

The then method is called if the promise is fulfilled, and logs the data to the console. The catch method is called if the promise is rejected, and logs the error to the console.

Async & Await

Async/await is a newer syntax introduced in ES6 that makes writing and managing asynchronous code in JavaScript much easier.

Asynchronous code is code that doesn't execute immediately, but at some later time, after some other code has finished executing. This is often used when making API requests or working with databases, as these operations can take a long time to complete.

Before async/await, developers had to use callback functions or promises to handle asynchronous code. While both of these methods work well, they can become hard to manage and lead to what's called "callback hell" when dealing with complex asynchronous code.

Async/await makes asynchronous code look and behave like synchronous code, which makes it much easier to read and understand. It uses the async and await keywords to achieve this.

Here's an example of using async/await to fetch data from an API:

```javascript
async function fetchUserData() {
  try {
    const response = await fetch('https://api.example.com/users');
    const data = await response.json();
    console.log(data);
  } catch (error) {
    console.error(error);
  }
}
```

In this example, we define an async function called fetchUserData. Inside the function, we use the await keyword to wait for the response from the API to be returned. We then use await again to convert the response to JSON data. Finally, we log the data to the console.

If there is an error during the API request or JSON conversion, we use the catch block to handle the error.

Dom Manipulation

The Document Object Model (DOM) is a tree-like structure that represents the web page in the browser.

We can use JavaScript to manipulate the DOM, which allows us to add, modify, and delete HTML elements and their attributes.

Here are some common ways to manipulate the DOM using JavaScript:

- Selecting Elements: We can select HTML elements using methods like getElementById(), getElementsByClassName(), and getElementsByTagName(). Here's an example:

```
let myElement = document.getElementById("myElementId");
myElement.innerHTML = "Hello, world!";
```

- Modifying Elements: Once we have selected an element, we can modify its properties like innerHTML, textContent, style, and classList. Here's an example:

```
let myElement = document.getElementById("myElementId");
myElement.style.color = "red";
myElement.classList.add("highlight");
```

Creating New Elements: We can create new HTML elements using the createElement() method, and then add them to the DOM using methods like appendChild() and insertBefore().

Here's an example:

```javascript
let newElement = document.createElement("p");
newElement.textContent = "This is a new paragraph!";
document.body.appendChild(newElement);
```

Event Handling: We can use JavaScript to handle events like mouse clicks, key presses, and form submissions. Here's an example:

```javascript
let myButton = document.getElementById("myButtonId");
myButton.addEventListener("click", function() {
  alert("Button clicked!");
});
```

DOM manipulation is a powerful tool in web development, and it's essential to have a good understanding of it if you want to create dynamic and interactive web pages.

JSON and Web Storage

JSON (JavaScript Object Notation) is a lightweight data interchange format that is easy for humans to read and write and easy for machines to parse and generate. In JavaScript, JSON is used to store and exchange data between a server and a web application.

To work with JSON in JavaScript, we can use the built-in JSON object. The JSON object has two methods, JSON.stringify() and JSON.parse(), that are commonly used for converting JavaScript objects to JSON and vice versa.

Here's an example of how to convert a JavaScript object to JSON:

```javascript
const person = {
  name: 'John',
  age: 30,
  email: 'john@example.com'
};

const json = JSON.stringify(person);

console.log(json);
// Output: {"name":"John","age":30,"email":"john@example.com"}
```

And here's an example of how to convert JSON to a JavaScript object:

```javascript
const json = '{"name":"John","age":30,"email":"john@example.com"}';

const person = JSON.parse(json);

console.log(person);
// Output: { name: 'John', age: 30, email: 'john@example.com' }
```

Web Storage is a way to store data in a web browser. There are two types of Web Storage - localStorage and sessionStorage. Both types of storage allow you to store data as key/value pairs.

Here's an example of how to use localStorage to store and retrieve data:

```
// Store data in localStorage
localStorage.setItem('name', 'John');
localStorage.setItem('age', '30');

// Retrieve data from localStorage
const name = localStorage.getItem('name');
const age = localStorage.getItem('age');

console.log(name, age);
// Output: John 30
```

And here's an example of how to use sessionStorage:

```
// Store data in sessionStorage
sessionStorage.setItem('name', 'John');
sessionStorage.setItem('age', '30');

// Retrieve data from sessionStorage
const name = sessionStorage.getItem('name');
const age = sessionStorage.getItem('age');

console.log(name, age);
// Output: John 30
```

Note that localStorage and sessionStorage can only store strings. To store and retrieve objects, you need to use JSON.stringify() and JSON.parse() as shown earlier.

Chapter 4 Project

Congratulations on making it through chapter 4! This chapter, you'll be building a fun and functional Todo application using HTML, CSS, and JavaScript. You'll also be making use of Local Storage to store your todos.

Here are the instructions:

- Start by creating an HTML page that contains a form to add a new Todo item, a list to display existing Todo items, and buttons to remove the Todo items.
- Use CSS to style the HTML page and make it visually appealing. You can use Bootstrap or Tailwind CSS to make it look even better!
- Use JavaScript to create an array that will store the todos. Each todo should have a unique ID and a text description.
- Use DOM manipulation to display the existing todos on the HTML page.
- Add an event listener to the "Add" button that will add a new todo item to the array and update the HTML page accordingly.
- Add event listeners to the "Remove" buttons that will remove the corresponding todo item from the array and update the HTML page accordingly.
- Use Local Storage to store the todos so that they persist even after the user closes the browser.

Make sure your Todo application is both functional and visually appealing! You can use your creativity to make it even more fun!

Remember to use Bootstrap or Tailwind CSS, as well as any other JavaScript concepts you've learned so far.

Good luck and have fun building your Todo application!

Ctrl + Shift + Frontend

CHAPTER 5

Welcome to chapter 5! This chapter, you will be learning about frontend frameworks, which are an essential part of modern web development. A frontend framework is a pre-written code that allows you to build complex user interfaces quickly and efficiently.

Frontend frameworks are particularly useful when developing large, complex web applications that require multiple pages or views. They provide a standardized way of organizing and structuring code, which can help with maintenance and scalability.

This chapter, you will have the option to choose between two popular frontend frameworks: React and Angular. Both of these frameworks are widely used in industry, and learning one of them will be a valuable addition to your skillset as a frontend developer. So, get ready to dive deep into the world of frontend frameworks!

Angular

(React Users can skip this section)

Angular is a popular frontend framework that is developed and maintained by Google. It is built on top of TypeScript, which is a superset of JavaScript, and provides a comprehensive set of tools and features for building complex, scalable, and maintainable web applications.

To get started with Angular, you need to have Node.js and npm (Node Package Manager) installed on your system. You can download and install them from the official Node.js website.

Once you have installed Node.js and npm, you can use the following command to install the Angular CLI (Command Line Interface) globally on your system:

Ctrl + Shift + Frontend

This will install the latest version of the Angular CLI on your system, which you can use to create and manage Angular projects.

To create a new Angular project, you can use the following command:

```
ng new my-app
```

This will create a new Angular project with the name "my-app" in the current directory. The Angular CLI will also install all the necessary dependencies and generate a basic project structure for you.

To run the blank Angular project, navigate to the project directory and use the following command:

```
cd my-app
ng serve
```

This will compile your Angular application and serve it on the default port (4200). You can then access your application by opening a web browser and navigating to http://localhost:4200 .Once you have set up the Angular environment and created a blank project, you can start building your own Angular application using the various features and components provided by the framework.

TypeScript Basics

TypeScript is a superset of JavaScript, which means that any valid JavaScript code is also valid TypeScript code. However, TypeScript offers additional features and syntax that can help developers write better code and catch errors earlier in the development process.

Some of the key features of TypeScript include:

- **Static Typing:** TypeScript supports static typing, which means that variables, parameters, and function return types can be assigned a specific data type at design time. This helps to catch errors earlier in the development process and makes code more readable and maintainable.
- **Classes and Interfaces:** TypeScript supports classes and interfaces, which are key features of object-oriented programming. Classes can be used to define objects with properties and methods, while interfaces can be used to define the shape of an object.
- **Type Inference:** TypeScript can infer the data type of a variable based on its value. This means that you don't always need to explicitly specify the data type of a variable.
- **Modules:** TypeScript supports modules, which allow you to organize code into reusable components. Modules can be used to define classes, functions, and variables that can be shared across multiple files.

Variable Declaration:

In TypeScript, we can use the let and const keywords for variable declaration just like in JavaScript.

Example:

```
let age: number = 25;
const name: string = "John";
```

Type Annotations:

TypeScript allows us to specify the type of a variable explicitly using the syntax: variable_name: type_name. This is called a type annotation.

Example:

```
let age: number = 25;
let name: string = "John";
```

Type Inference:

TypeScript also infers types automatically based on the value assigned to the variable. This is called type inference.

Example:

```
let age = 25; // TypeScript infers the type as number
let name = "John"; // TypeScript infers the type as string
```

Interfaces:

Interfaces are used to define the structure of an object in TypeScript. They are used to enforce a contract between different parts of the code.

Example:

```
interface Person {
    name: string;
    age: number;
}

let person: Person = {
    name: "John",
    age: 25
};
```

Classes:

Classes in TypeScript are used to define objects with methods and properties. They can be used to create reusable code.

Example:

```typescript
class Person {
  name: string;
  age: number;

  constructor(name: string, age: number) {
    this.name = name;
    this.age = age;
  }

  getInfo() {
    return `Name: ${this.name}, Age: ${this.age}`;
  }
}

let person = new Person("John", 25);
console.log(person.getInfo());
```

Enumerations:

Enumerations are used to define a set of named constants.

Example:

```typescript
enum Color {
  Red,
  Green,
  Blue
}

let color: Color = Color.Green;
console.log(color); // Output: 1
```

Union Types:

Union types allow a variable to have more than one possible type.

Example:

```
let id: string | number = 123;
id = "abc";
```

Folder Structure

node_modules: This folder contains all the dependencies and packages that the project needs. It's automatically generated when you run npm install.

src: This folder contains the source code for the project. It includes the main application code, assets, styles, and tests.

app: This folder contains the main application code. It includes components, services, modules, and other related files.

components: This folder contains all the components used in the application. Each component is a separate folder containing a .ts file, .html file, and .css file.

services: This folder contains all the services used in the application. A service is a singleton object that provides some functionality to the components.

modules: This folder contains all the modules used in the application. A module is a container for related components, directives, pipes, and services.

app-routing.module.ts: This file contains the routing configuration for the application.

app.component.ts: This file contains the main component for the application.

assets: This folder contains all the static assets used in the application such as images, fonts, and other files.

styles.css: This file contains the global styles for the application.

index.html: This file is the main entry point for the application.

angular.json: This file contains the configuration for the Angular CLI.

package.json: This file contains the dependencies and scripts for the project.

tsconfig.json: This file contains the configuration for the TypeScript compiler.

tslint.json: This file contains the rules for the TypeScript linter.

README.md: This file contains the documentation for the project.

The folder structure may vary based on the specific needs of the project, but the above structure is commonly used in most Angular projects.

Component

In Angular, a component is the fundamental building block of an application. It is responsible for the application's UI and consists of three parts:

- **Template:** This is the view that users see. It contains the HTML, CSS, and Angular directives that define how the UI should be displayed.
- **Class:** This is the logic that defines the component's behavior. It contains the properties and methods that define how the component should behave, and it interacts with the view through bindings.
- **Metadata:** This is the extra information that Angular needs to know about the component, such as its selector, template, and styles.

Here's an example of a simple Angular component structure:

Ctrl + Shift + Frontend

```
import { Component } from '@angular/core';

@Component({
  selector: 'app-example',
  template: `
    <h1>{{ title }}</h1>
    <p>{{ message }}</p>
  `,
  styles: [`
    h1 {
      color: blue;
    }
    p {
      font-size: 18px;
    }
  `]
})
export class ExampleComponent {
  title = 'Example Component';
  message = 'This is an example of an Angular component.';
}
```

Overall, the component structure in Angular follows the Model-View-Controller (MVC) pattern, where the component class acts as the controller, the template acts as the view, and the metadata provides additional information to help Angular create and use the component.

Here's an example of how to create a simple component in Angular:

Create a new component using the Angular CLI command:

```
ng generate component my-component
```

This will create a new folder named my-component in the src/app directory with the following files:

my-component.component.ts: TypeScript file that defines the component logic.
my-component.component.html: HTML template file that defines the component's UI.
my-component.component.css: CSS file that defines the component's styles.

my-component.component.spec.ts: TypeScript file that contains the unit tests for the component.

Open the my-component.component.ts file and define the component class:

```typescript
import { Component } from '@angular/core';

@Component({
  selector: 'app-my-component',
  templateUrl: './my-component.component.html',
  styleUrls: ['./my-component.component.css']
})
export class MyComponent {
  title = 'My Component';
}
```

Here, we import the Component decorator from @angular/core and use it to define the component metadata. The selector property defines the component's tag name, which we can use to include the component in other templates. The templateUrl property specifies the HTML template file for the component, and the styleUrls property specifies the CSS file(s) for the component. Finally, we define the component class with a title property.

Open the my-component.component.html file and define the component's UI:

```html
<h1>{{ title }}</h1>
```

Here, we use the {{ }} syntax to interpolate the value of the title property from the component class into the HTML template.

Use the component in another template:

Here, we include the my-component tag in another template to render the component's UI.

That's it! This is a basic example of how to create and use a component in Angular.

Templates

In Angular, a template is used to create the user interface of an application. It is essentially an HTML file that includes Angular-specific syntax and directives to dynamically render data and provide interactivity.

A basic Angular template consists of HTML elements and Angular-specific syntax, such as binding expressions, event binding, and structural directives. For example, you can use the double curly braces notation {{}} to display data from a component property in a template.

Here's an example of a basic Angular template:

In the example above, we're using the double curly braces notation to bind the title and message properties of a component to HTML elements in the template.

Templates can be included inline in a component's metadata or in a separate file. To include a separate template file, you use the templateUrl property in the component's metadata.

Here is an example of an inline template:

```
@Component({
  selector: 'app-my-component',
  template: `
    <div>
      <h1>Hello {{ name }}</h1>
    </div>
  `,
})
export class MyComponent {
  name = 'John';
}
```

In this example, we have defined an inline template for a component called MyComponent. The template includes an expression that evaluates to the name property on the component, which is set to 'John'.

Here is an example of a template file:

```
@Component({
  selector: 'app-my-component',
  templateUrl: './my-component.component.html',
})
export class MyComponent {
  name = 'John';
}
```

Angular templates can also include directives, which are used to apply custom behavior to HTML elements. For example, the ngFor directive can be used to iterate over a list and create a dynamic list of elements. Here is an example:

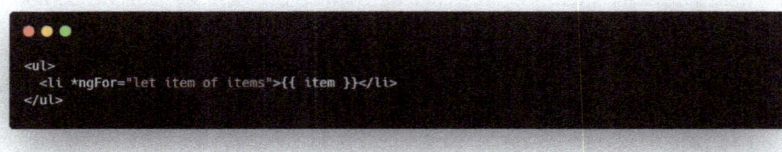

In this example, we are using the ngFor directive to create a list of items. The *ngFor syntax is known as a structural directive, because it can add or remove elements from the DOM based on the contents of the list.

Angular templates are a powerful tool for creating dynamic user interfaces. With the ability to include expressions and directives, you can create complex layouts and behaviors with ease.

Services

Services in Angular are classes that provide functionality to components throughout an application. Services can be used to perform tasks such as fetching data from an API, handling user authentication, and managing state.

Creating a Service in Angular is simple. You can use the Angular CLI to generate a new Service:

This will create a new Service file called my-service.service.ts in the src/app folder.

The generated Service will have an empty @Injectable() decorator, which is required for Angular to inject the Service into other components:

```
import { Injectable } from '@angular/core';

@Injectable({
  providedIn: 'root'
})
export class MyServiceService {

  constructor() { }

}
```

In the Service class, you can define methods that perform specific tasks, such as fetching data from an API

In the example below, the getData() method uses the HttpClient module from Angular's @angular/common/http package to make an HTTP request to an API endpoint.

```
import { Injectable } from '@angular/core';
import { HttpClient } from '@angular/common/http';

@Injectable({
  providedIn: 'root'
})
export class MyServiceService {

  constructor(private http: HttpClient) { }

  getData() {
    return this.http.get('https://jsonplaceholder.typicode.com/posts');
  }

}
```

To use a Service in a component, you need to inject it into the component's constructor:

```
import { Component } from '@angular/core';
import { MyServiceService } from './my-service.service';

@Component({
  selector: 'app-my-component',
  template: '<p>{{ data }}</p>'
})
export class MyComponentComponent {

  data: any;

  constructor(private myService: MyServiceService) { }

  ngOnInit() {
    this.myService.getData().subscribe((result) => {
      this.data = result;
    });
  }
}
```

In the example above, the MyComponentComponent uses the MyServiceService to fetch data from an API and display it in the component's template.

That's a basic overview of Services in Angular. By using Services, you can share data and functionality across different components in your application, making your code more modular and easier to maintain.

Directives

Directives are a way to add custom behavior to HTML elements in Angular applications. There are three types of directives in Angular:

- Component Directives: A component directive is a directive that has its own template and its own view. A component is a directive with a template.
- Attribute Directives: An attribute directive is a directive that changes the appearance or behavior of an element by adding, removing, or modifying attributes. Attribute directives are applied to elements as attributes.
- Structural Directives: A structural directive is a directive that changes the structure of the DOM by adding, removing, or manipulating elements. Structural directives are applied to elements as attributes, but they can add, remove, or manipulate elements that are not present in the original DOM.

Here's an example of an attribute directive that changes the background color of an element:

```typescript
import { Directive, ElementRef, Input } from '@angular/core';

@Directive({
  selector: '[appHighlight]'
})
export class HighlightDirective {
  constructor(private el: ElementRef) { }

  @Input() highlightColor: string;

  ngOnInit() {
    this.el.nativeElement.style.backgroundColor = this.highlightColor || 'yellow';
  }
}
```

In this example, the @Directive decorator is used to define a new directive named HighlightDirective. The selector property is set to '[appHighlight]', which means that this directive will be applied to any element that has the appHighlight attribute.

The constructor method injects the ElementRef service, which provides access to the DOM element that this directive is attached to.

The @Input decorator is used to define an input property named highlightColor, which can be used to specify the background color of the element.

The ngOnInit method is called when the directive is initialized. In this method, we set the background color of the element using the nativeElement property of the ElementRef object.

To use this directive in a template, you would simply add the appHighlight attribute to an element and optionally specify the highlightColor input property:

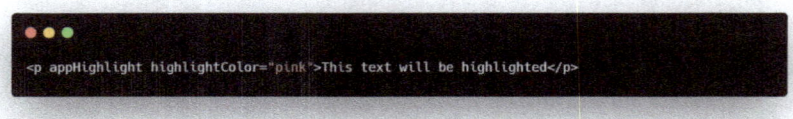

This will apply the HighlightDirective to the p element and set its background color to pink.

In conclusion, directives are a powerful tool in Angular that enable you to manipulate the DOM and apply custom behavior to HTML elements. With directives, you can extend the functionality of HTML tags, create reusable components, and add custom logic to your application. Whether you need to change the appearance of an element, bind data to it, or listen for events, directives provide a flexible and efficient way to achieve your goals. By mastering directives, you can greatly enhance the capabilities of your Angular applications and create more sophisticated and dynamic user interfaces.

Dependency Injection

Dependency Injection (DI) is a design pattern that is used to achieve Inversion of Control (IoC) in software applications. In Angular, DI is used to provide dependencies to components at runtime. It allows us to create reusable code that can be injected into different components without coupling them together. DI makes our code more modular, easier to test and maintain.

In Angular, the DI system is built-in and is responsible for creating and providing instances of services, components, pipes, and other types of objects to the rest of the application. When we declare a provider, we are telling Angular how to create and provide an instance of a particular object. We can also use the @Injectable decorator to make a class injectable and use the constructor to declare its dependencies.

To use DI in Angular, we need to follow these steps:

- Declare the dependency: We declare the dependency by specifying it as a constructor parameter.
- Create a provider: We create a provider that will be responsible for creating and providing the dependency.
- Register the provider: We register the provider with the Angular injector.

- Use the dependency: We use the dependency in our code by calling its methods or accessing its properties.

Here's an example of how to use DI in Angular:

```
import { Component } from '@angular/core';
import { MyService } from './my-service';

@Component({
  selector: 'my-component',
  template: `
    <h1>{{ message }}</h1>
  `,
  providers: [MyService]
})
export class MyComponent {
  message: string;

  constructor(private myService: MyService) {
    this.message = myService.getMessage();
  }
}
```

Routing

Routing in Angular refers to the process of defining routes or paths for different views or components in an application. It allows you to create a single-page application with multiple views or pages without the need for a full page refresh.

In Angular, you can define routes using the RouterModule, which provides a set of directives for navigation, including:

- RouterLink: A directive that binds a clickable HTML element to a route.
- RouterLinkActive: A directive that adds a CSS class to an HTML element when the corresponding route is active.
- RouterOutlet: A directive that acts as a placeholder where the router can insert the component for the corresponding route.

To use routing in Angular, you need to define the routes for your application. This can be done by importing the RouterModule and using the forRoot() method to define your routes:

```
import { RouterModule, Routes } from '@angular/router';
import { HomeComponent } from './home/home.component';
import { AboutComponent } from './about/about.component';

const routes: Routes = [
  { path: '', component: HomeComponent },
  { path: 'about', component: AboutComponent },
];

@NgModule({
  imports: [RouterModule.forRoot(routes)],
  exports: [RouterModule]
})
export class AppRoutingModule { }
```

In the example above, we define two routes: one for the HomeComponent and one for the AboutComponent. The empty path ('') corresponds to the HomeComponent, and the path '/about' corresponds to the AboutComponent.

Once you have defined your routes, you can use the RouterLink directive in your HTML templates to navigate to different routes:

```
<nav>
  <a routerLink="/">Home</a>
  <a routerLink="/about">About</a>
</nav>

<router-outlet></router-outlet>
```

In the example above, we define a navigation menu with two links that use the RouterLink directive to navigate to the HomeComponent and the AboutComponent. The RouterOutlet directive is used as a placeholder where the corresponding component will be rendered.

Overall, Routing is an essential concept in Angular that allows you to create a single-page application with multiple views or pages. With the RouterModule and its set of directives, you can easily define and navigate between different routes in your application.

Forms

The next topic after routing is forms in Angular. Forms are an essential part of any web application, and Angular provides a powerful way to create and work with forms. Angular forms come with features like validation, data binding, and reactive programming that make them a popular choice for creating forms.

In Angular, forms can be created using two approaches: template-driven forms and reactive forms. Template-driven forms are based on two-way data binding, whereas reactive forms are based on reactive programming using the RxJS library.

Template-driven forms are easy to use and require minimal code, making them an excellent choice for simple forms. They are created using the ngForm directive and ngModel directive to create form controls.

Reactive forms, on the other hand, provide more control and flexibility when working with complex forms. They use the FormBuilder service to create form controls and enable reactive programming using the RxJS library. Reactive forms provide better control over form validation and data flow and are the preferred choice for complex forms.

In addition to template-driven and reactive forms, Angular also provides built-in validators that can be used to validate form inputs. Validators can be used to ensure that form inputs meet specific requirements, such as minimum and maximum length, required fields, and pattern matching.

Overall, Angular forms provide a powerful way to create and work with forms in web applications, and learning how to use them is essential for any Angular developer.

Ctrl + Shift + Frontend

```html
<form>
  <label>
    Name:
    <input type="text" name="name" [(ngModel)]="name">
  </label>
  <br>
  <label>
    Email:
    <input type="email" name="email" [(ngModel)]="email">
  </label>
  <br>
  <button type="submit" (click)="submitForm()">Submit</button>
</form>
```

In the component file, we can define the name and email variables and the submitForm() method to handle form submission:

```typescript
import { Component } from '@angular/core';

@Component({
  selector: 'app-form',
  templateUrl: './form.component.html',
  styleUrls: ['./form.component.css']
})
export class FormComponent {
  name: string;
  email: string;

  submitForm() {
    console.log(`Name: ${this.name}, Email: ${this.email}`);
  }
}
```

```html
<form [formGroup]="myForm" (ngSubmit)="onSubmit()">
  <label>
    Name:
    <input type="text" formControlName="name">
    <div *ngIf="myForm.controls.name.invalid && (myForm.controls.name.dirty || myForm.controls.name.touched)">
      <div *ngIf="myForm.controls.name.errors.required">Name is required.</div>
      <div *ngIf="myForm.controls.name.errors.minlength">Name must be at least {{ myForm.controls.name.errors.minlength.requiredLength }} characters.</div>
    </div>
  </label>
  <label>
    Email:
    <input type="email" formControlName="email">
    <div *ngIf="myForm.controls.email.invalid && (myForm.controls.email.dirty || myForm.controls.email.touched)">
      <div *ngIf="myForm.controls.email.errors.required">Email is required.</div>
      <div *ngIf="myForm.controls.email.errors.email">Email must be a valid email address.</div>
    </div>
  </label>
  <button type="submit" [disabled]="!myForm.valid">Submit</button>
</form>
```

In this example, we're adding validation messages to our form using ngIf and checking for specific errors on the form controls. We're also using properties such as dirty and touch to control when the validation messages are displayed. These are just a few examples of how to use Angular forms. There are many more features and options available, such as form arrays and custom validators, that can be explored further.

Observables and Pipes

Observables and pipes are two powerful features of Angular that are used to work with asynchronous data and transform data in an Angular application.

Observables are a key part of Angular's RxJS library, which provides a powerful way to work with asynchronous data in Angular applications. Observables are used to handle asynchronous operations such as HTTP requests or events, and provide a way to subscribe to the results of these operations.

Observable objects represent a stream of data that can be observed by one or more subscribers. The stream can emit a series of values over time, and can also emit an error or complete notification.

Observable values can be transformed using various operators provided by the RxJS library. Operators such as map(), filter(), and debounceTime() can be used to modify the stream of data emitted by an observable.

Here's an example of using an observable to fetch data from an API and subscribe to the results:

```typescript
import { Component, OnInit } from '@angular/core';
import { HttpClient } from '@angular/common/http';
import { Observable } from 'rxjs';

@Component({
  selector: 'app-example',
  template: `
    <ul>
      <li *ngFor="let item of items">{{ item }}</li>
    </ul>
  `
})
export class ExampleComponent implements OnInit {
  items$: Observable<any>;

  constructor(private http: HttpClient) {}

  ngOnInit() {
    this.items$ = this.http.get('https://jsonplaceholder.typicode.com/todos');
    this.items$.subscribe(
      data => console.log(data),
      error => console.error(error),
      () => console.log('Request complete')
    );
  }
}
```

In this example, we use the HttpClient module to make an HTTP GET request to an API and return an observable stream of data. We then subscribe to this stream using the subscribe() method and handle the emitted data, error, and complete notifications.

Pipes are a feature in Angular that allow us to transform data in a template expression. Pipes can be used to format data, filter data, or sort data in a template expression without changing the underlying data.

Angular provides several built-in pipes, such as date, uppercase, and lowercase, as well as the ability to create custom pipes.

Here's an example of using the built-in date pipe to format a date:

```html
<p>{{ date | date:'MM/dd/yyyy' }}</p>
```

In this example, we use the date pipe to format a date string in a template expression. The pipe takes the date string and formats it to the specified format.

We can also create custom pipes to transform data in a template expression. In this example, we create a custom pipe called 'filter' that takes an array of objects and a search term as arguments. The pipe then filters the array based on the search term and returns the filtered array.

```typescript
import { Pipe, PipeTransform } from '@angular/core';

@Pipe({ name: 'filter' })
export class FilterPipe implements PipeTransform {
  transform(items: any[], searchText: string): any[] {
    if (!items) return [];
    if (!searchText) return items;
    searchText = searchText.toLowerCase();
    return items.filter(item => {
      return item.name.toLowerCase().includes(searchText);
    });
  }
}
```

Ctrl + Shift + Frontend

React

React is a popular JavaScript library for building user interfaces. It was created by Facebook and is now widely used by developers all over the world. React makes it easy to create reusable UI components and efficiently render them to the DOM. It is also known for its efficient rendering and performance optimization, making it a great choice for building complex applications with a lot of user interactions. In addition, React has a large and active community with plenty of resources available for developers to learn from and use in their projects.

Getting Started

React is a JavaScript library for building user interfaces, and it uses a syntax called JSX to create and manipulate DOM elements. Here are the steps to get started with React:

Install Node.js: React requires Node.js to run, so you'll need to download and install it on your computer if you don't already have it.

Create a new React project: Once you have Node.js installed, you can use the command-line tool "create-react-app" to create a new React project. Open your terminal and run the following command:

```
npx create-react-app my-app
```

Replace "my-app" with the name of your project.

Run the development server: Once your project is created, navigate to the project directory in your terminal and run the following command to start the development server:

```
npm start
```

Ctrl + Shift + Frontend

This will start a development server that will automatically refresh your browser as you make changes to your code.

Begin coding: Now that you have your development server running, you're ready to start coding your React app. The entry point for your app is the "index.js" file located in the "src" directory. You can start creating your React components in separate files and importing them into the "index.js" file.

That's it! With these steps, you can start building your first React app.

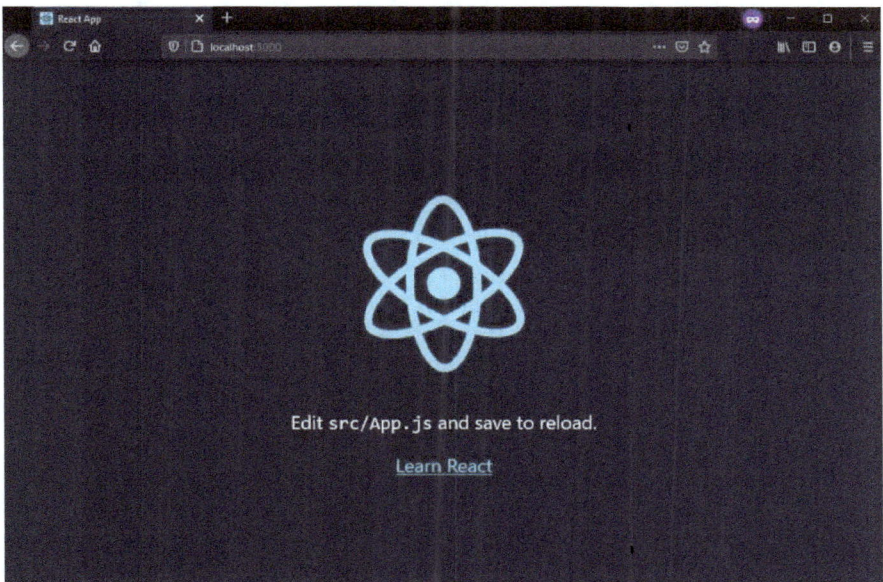

Ctrl + Shift + Frontend

File Structure

- **node_modules/:** This folder contains all the dependencies installed by npm, which is used to manage packages in Node.js projects.
- **public/:** This folder contains the static assets that will be served by the server. The index.html file is the main HTML file that will be loaded by the browser, and favicon.ico is the icon displayed in the browser tab.
- **src/:** This folder contains the source code for the React application. App.js is the main React component, App.css contains styles for the App component, index.js is the entry point for the application, and index.css contains global styles for the application.
- **package.json:** This file contains metadata about the project and a list of its dependencies.
- **package-lock.json:** This file is generated by npm to lock down the versions of dependencies that were installed.
- **README.md:** This file contains information about the project and instructions on how to use it.
- **.gitignore:** This file lists files and directories that should be ignored by Git version control.

This is a basic folder structure and can be customized according to the specific needs of the project.

Ctrl + Shift + Frontend

Virtual Dom

The Virtual DOM is a concept in React that enables efficient updates to the user interface by minimizing the number of changes required to update the DOM. In a traditional web application, when a user interacts with the UI, the browser re-renders the entire page to reflect the change. This process can be slow and resource-intensive, especially when dealing with complex user interfaces.

React's Virtual DOM works by creating an in-memory representation of the actual DOM called the Virtual DOM. When a user interacts with the UI, React updates the Virtual DOM instead of the actual DOM. It then compares the updated Virtual DOM with the previous version to determine the minimum number of changes required to update the actual DOM. Finally, it applies only those changes to the actual DOM, resulting in a much faster and efficient update process . React's Virtual DOM also enables developers to write code in a declarative manner, where they describe what the UI should look like for a given state, rather than how to update the UI. This approach makes it easier to reason about the code and reduces the chances of introducing bugs.

Overall, the Virtual DOM is a powerful concept in React that enables developers to create efficient and scalable user interfaces with minimal effort.

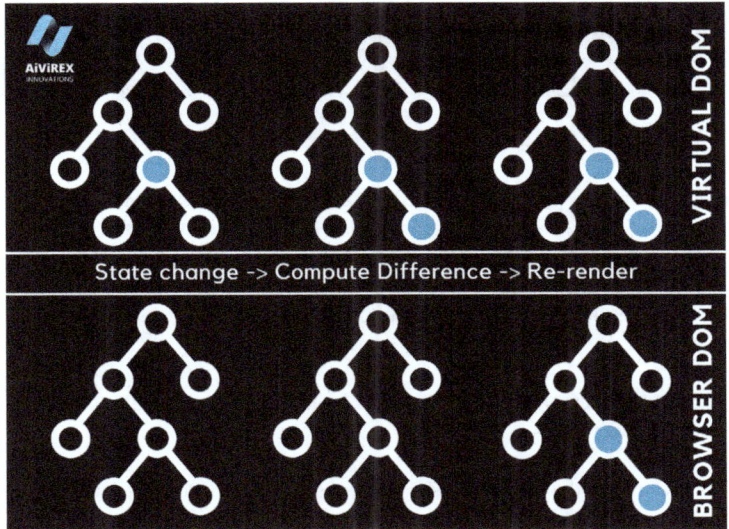

JSX

JSX (JavaScript XML) is an extension of JavaScript syntax that allows us to write HTML-like code in our JavaScript code.

It makes it easy to create and manipulate the UI components in React. JSX syntax is not valid JavaScript code and it must be transpiled to regular JavaScript code before it can be run in the browser.

Here's an example of how to use JSX in a React component:

```jsx
import React from 'react';

function App() {
  return (
    <div className="App">
      <h1>Hello, World!</h1>
      <p>This is a paragraph.</p>
    </div>
  );
}

export default App;
```

In the above example, we are using JSX to create a div element with a class name of "App", and inside it we have an h1 element with the text "Hello, World!" and a p element with the text "This is a paragraph.".

Note that we are using className instead of class to add a class name to the div element.

This is because class is a reserved keyword in JavaScript, and we cannot use it as an attribute name in JSX.

Also, the code inside the return statement looks like HTML, but it is actually JSX. The transpiler will convert this JSX code into regular JavaScript code that creates and manipulates the UI components.

Hooks

React Hooks are a new addition to the React library that allows developers to use state and other React features without writing a class component.

There are several built-in hooks that are frequently used in React applications.

useState(): useState is the most frequently used hook that allows you to add state to functional components. It takes an initial state value as an argument and returns an array containing two values: the current state value and a function to update the state.

Here's an example of using useState to update a counter:

```jsx
import React, { useState } from 'react';

function Counter() {
  const [count, setCount] = useState(0);

  return (
    <div>
      <p>You clicked {count} times</p>
      <button onClick={() => setCount(count + 1)}>
        Click me
      </button>
    </div>
  );
}
```

useEffect(): useEffect is another frequently used hook that allows you to perform side effects in functional components.

It takes a function as an argument and runs it after every render.

You can also specify a dependency array to control when the effect should be run. Here's an example of using useEffect to fetch data from an API:

```
import React, { useState, useEffect } from 'react';
import axios from 'axios';

function UserList() {
  const [users, setUsers] = useState([]);

  useEffect(() => {
    axios.get('https://jsonplaceholder.typicode.com/users')
      .then(response => {
        setUsers(response.data);
      })
      .catch(error => {
        console.log(error);
      });
  }, []);

  return (
    <ul>
      {users.map(user => (
        <li key={user.id}>{user.name}</li>
      ))}
    </ul>
  );
}
```

useContext(): useContext is a hook that allows you to consume a context in a functional component. It takes a context object as an argument and returns the current value of the context.

Here's an example of using useContext to access a theme context:

```
import React, { useContext } from 'react';
import ThemeContext from './ThemeContext';

function Header() {
  const theme = useContext(ThemeContext);

  return (
    <header style={{ backgroundColor: theme.background }}>
      <h1 style={{ color: theme.foreground }}>My App</h1>
    </header>
  );
}
```

useRef(): useRef is a hook that allows you to create a mutable reference that persists across renders.

You can use it to access DOM elements or to store any other mutable value. Here's an example of using useRef to focus an input field:

```jsx
import React, { useRef } from 'react';

function InputWithFocusButton() {
  const inputRef = useRef(null);

  function handleClick() {
    inputRef.current.focus();
  }

  return (
    <div>
      <input type="text" ref={inputRef} />
      <button onClick={handleClick}>Focus</button>
    </div>
  );
}
```

These are just a few examples of the many hooks available in React. By using hooks, developers can write functional components that are more concise and easier to understand than class components.

Unidirectional Data Binding

In React, data flows unidirectionally, meaning that the data always flows in a single direction, from parent components to child components. This is known as unidirectional data binding, or one-way data flow.

To implement unidirectional data binding, we pass data as props from parent components to child components. When the data changes in the parent component, the updated data is passed down to the child component as props. The child component can then use the updated data to re-render itself.

Here is an example of how unidirectional data binding works in React:

```
import React, { useState } from 'react';

function ParentComponent() {
  const [count, setCount] = useState(0);

  return (
    <div>
      <h2>Parent Component</h2>
      <p>Count: {count}</p>
      <ChildComponent count={count} />
      <button onClick={() => setCount(count + 1)}>Increment Count</button>
    </div>
  );
}

function ChildComponent(props) {
  return (
    <div>
      <h2>Child Component</h2>
      <p>Count: {props.count}</p>
    </div>
  );
}
```

In this example, we have a ParentComponent that maintains a count state using the useState hook. The count value is passed down to the ChildComponent as a prop. When the count value is incremented by clicking the "Increment Count" button in the ParentComponent, the updated count value is passed down to the ChildComponent as props, causing it to re-render with the new count value.

This is a simple example of how unidirectional data binding works in React, and how it can be used to pass data from parent components to child components.

Forms

To handle forms in React, you can use the useState hook to store the input values in the component state and the onSubmit event to handle the form submission.

Here's an example of a simple form component that takes an input value and logs it in the console when the form is submitted:

```jsx
import React, { useState } from 'react';

function Form() {
  const [inputValue, setInputValue] = useState('');

  const handleSubmit = (event) => {
    event.preventDefault();
    console.log(inputValue);
  };

  return (
    <form onSubmit={handleSubmit}>
      <label>
        Input value:
        <input
          type="text"
          value={inputValue}
          onChange={((event) => setInputValue(event.target.value)}
        />
      </label>
      <button type="submit">Submit</button>
    </form>
  );
}

export default Form;
```

In this example, we use the useState hook to create a state variable called inputValue and a function called setInputValue to update the state. The value prop of the input element is set to the inputValue state, and the onChange event updates the inputValue state when the user types in the input field. The handleSubmit function is called when the form is submitted, and it prevents the default form submission behavior using event.preventDefault(). It then logs the inputValue state in the console. Finally, we render a form element with a label and an input field. The onSubmit event is set to call the handleSubmit function, and a button element is added to submit the form.

With this example, you can handle forms in React and store the input values in the component state. You can also customize the form submission behavior to fit your needs.

Components

In React, components are the building blocks of the UI. They are reusable, composable, and encapsulated, which means that they can be combined in various ways to create complex user interfaces.

Components can be divided into two types: functional components and class components.

Functional components are simpler and easier to read and write than class components.

They are also known as stateless components because they do not have any state of their own.

Functional components take in props, which are plain JavaScript objects containing the data that the component needs to render. They then return what should be rendered to the DOM. Here's an example of a functional component:

```
import React from 'react';

function Greeting(props) {
  return <h1>Hello, {props.name}!</h1>;
}

export default Greeting;
```

Class components are more complex than functional components. They are also known as stateful components because they can hold state within themselves. Class components must extend the React.Component class, and they must have a render() method that returns the component's markup.

Routing

Routing is a fundamental feature of any single-page application (SPA), and with the latest updates in React Router, handling routing has become even more intuitive and streamlined.

In the newest version of React Router, the approach is simplified, allowing for easy route management without the need for <Switch>. Instead, you can use the <Routes> component to wrap your route definitions, ensuring that only the first matching route gets rendered.

Ctrl + Shift + Frontend

To get started, you'll first need to install React Router using NPM or Yarn:

```
npm install react-router-dom
```

Once installed, you can import the necessary components and set up your routes seamlessly. Here's an updated example of how to define routes in your application:

```
// put your codeimport { BrowserRouter as Router, Routes, Route } from 'react-router-dom';
import Home from './Home';
import About from './About';
import Contact from './Contact';

function App() {
  return (
    <Router>
      <Routes>
        <Route path="/" element={<Home />} />
        <Route path="/about" element={<About />} />
        <Route path="/contact" element={<Contact />} />
      </Routes>
    </Router>
  );
}
here
```

In this example, we've defined three routes for our application: the root route (`/`), the About page (`/about`), and the Contact page (`/contact`). Each route is linked to its respective component using the `element` prop, making it straightforward to manage navigation.

This new routing structure is not only cleaner but also enhances readability and maintainability. With React Router's latest version, you can easily add more features, such as URL parameters and nested routes, as your application grows. For instance, you can define dynamic segments in your routes to capture user input, making your application more interactive and responsive.

Moreover, React Router allows you to implement lazy loading of components. This means you can load components only when they are needed, improving the performance of your application and providing a better user experience by reducing initial load times.

Another great feature is the ability to implement route protection easily. By wrapping your routes with custom logic, you can restrict access to certain parts of your application based on user authentication status, adding an extra layer of security.

Overall, the latest version of React Router offers a powerful and flexible solution for managing routing in your React applications.

With just a few lines of code, you can define your routes and handle navigation seamlessly, ensuring a smooth and intuitive user experience.

The combination of these features allows developers to create scalable, maintainable, and user-friendly applications efficiently.

Higher Order Components

Higher-order components (HOCs) are a powerful feature in React that allow you to reuse component logic across your application. An HOC is a function that takes a component and returns a new component with additional functionality.

To create an HOC, you can define a function that takes a component as an argument, and returns a new component that wraps the original component.

The new component can then pass additional props or modify the behavior of the wrapped component in some way.

Here's an example of an HOC that logs the props of a component whenever it's rendered:

```
function withLogging(Component) {
  return function(props) {
    console.log("Props:", props);
    return <Component {...props} />;
  };
}

function MyComponent(props) {
  return <div>Hello, {props.name}!</div>;
}

const WrappedComponent = withLogging(MyComponent);

function App() {
  return <WrappedComponent name="Alice" />;
}
```

In this example, the withLogging function takes a Component as an argument, and returns a new function that logs the props of the component before rendering it. The new function returns the original component with its props spread onto it.

We then use the withLogging function to create a new component called WrappedComponent, which we pass to the App component with some props. When the WrappedComponent is rendered, the HOC logs the props to the console before rendering the original component with the props passed to it.

HOCs can be useful for a variety of use cases, such as providing authentication, managing state, or adding additional functionality to components. They're a powerful tool for creating reusable and composable components in React.

React Context

React Context is a way to pass data down the component tree without having to pass props down manually at every level.

It provides a way to share data between components that are not directly related to each other in the component tree. The Context API allows you to create a global state that can be accessed from anywhere in your application.

Here is an example of how to create and use a context:

```
// Create a context
const MyContext = React.createContext();

// Create a provider component
function MyProvider(props) {
  const [count, setCount] = useState(0);

  return (
    <MyContext.Provider value={{ count, setCount }}>
      {props.children}
    </MyContext.Provider>
  );
}

// Create a consumer component
function MyConsumer() {
  return (
    <MyContext.Consumer>
      {({ count, setCount }) => (
        <div>
          <p>Count: {count}</p>
          <button onClick={() => setCount(count + 1)}>Increment</button>
        </div>
      )}
    </MyContext.Consumer>
  );
}

// Use the provider and consumer in your app
function App() {
  return (
    <MyProvider>
      <div>
        <h1>My App</h1>
        <MyConsumer />
      </div>
    </MyProvider>
  );
}
```

To create a context, you can use the createContext() function provided by React. This function returns an object with two components: a Provider and a Consumer.

The Provider is used to wrap the part of the component tree where you want to share the data, and the Consumer is used to access the data from any child component.

In this example, the MyContext object is created using createContext(). The MyProvider component is then created, which wraps the child components that need access to the context data.

In this case, we are creating a state variable count and a function to update it setCount, which are passed to the value prop of the Provider.

The MyConsumer component is used to access the data from the context. It uses the Consumer component provided by MyContext, which accepts a function as a child.

This function receives the context data as an argument and returns the JSX that should be rendered.

Finally, we use the MyProvider component in our App component to wrap the components that need access to the context data.

The MyConsumer component is then used to display the data in the UI and to update the count state variable when the button is clicked.

React Context is a powerful feature that can simplify the management of global state in your application.

However, be careful not to overuse it, as it can lead to a complex and difficult-to-understand codebase if not used appropriately.

Styling

React offers multiple options for styling your application, including inline styling, external CSS files, CSS modules, and CSS-in-JS libraries. Let's explore each of these options:

Inline Styling: You can use inline styling in React by passing a style object to the JSX element's style attribute. The style object should contain CSS properties as key-value pairs. Here is an example:

```
const myStyle = {
    color: 'blue',
    backgroundColor: 'lightgrey',
    padding: '10px',
    border: '1px solid black'
};
function MyComponent() {
    return (
        <div style={myStyle}>
            This text is styled inline.
        </div>
    );
}
```

```
// myStyle.css
.myStyle {
  color: blue;
  background-color: lightgrey;
  padding: 10px;
  border: 1px solid black;
}

// MyComponent.js
import './myStyle.css';

function MyComponent() {
  return (
    <div className="myStyle">
      This text is styled using an external CSS file.
    </div>
  );
}
```

External CSS files: You can also create a separate CSS file and import it into your component. This is the traditional way of styling in web development.

CSS Modules: CSS modules are a way of locally scoped CSS. You can create a separate CSS file and import it into your component using the import statement. Then you can access the CSS class names as properties of the imported module. Here is an example:

```
// myStyle.module.css
.myStyle {
  color: blue;
  background-color: lightgrey;
  padding: 10px;
  border: 1px solid black;
}

// MyComponent.js
import styles from './myStyle.module.css';

function MyComponent() {
  return (
    <div className={styles.myStyle}>
      This text is styled using CSS modules.
    </div>
  );
}
```

These are some of the options available for styling your React application. Choose the one that best suits your project requirements and coding style.

Additionally, CSS frameworks like Tailwind and Bootstrap can also be used with React. To use Tailwind with React, you can install the tailwind css package and configure it using a tailwind.config.js file. You can then import Tailwind styles in your components using import './styles.css', where styles.css contains your Tailwind classes.

To use Bootstrap with React, you can install the react-bootstrap package, which provides pre-built React components styled with Bootstrap. Alternatively, you can install the bootstrap package and use it with React as you would with any other HTML project.

Chapter 5 Project

Project Title : Expense Tracker

The goal of this project is to build an expense tracker application using React and a CSS framework like Bootstrap or Tailwind. The application will allow users to add and delete expenses, view a list of their expenses, and view a total of all their expenses.

The application should have the following features:

- A form for adding new expenses with the fields "name", "amount", and "date".
- A list of all expenses, displaying the name, amount, and date of each expense.
- The ability to delete expenses from the list.
- A total expense amount displayed at the bottom of the list.
- The ability to save expenses to local storage, so that they persist across page reloads.

You can use the following array of dummy data as a starting point:

```
const expenses = [
  { id: 1, name: "Coffee", amount: 2.5, date: "2022-03-01" },
  { id: 2, name: "Lunch", amount: 12.75, date: "2022-03-01" },
  { id: 3, name: "Gas", amount: 35.0, date: "2022-02-28" },
];
```

- Create a new React or Angular application using create-react-app or your preferred method.
- Install a CSS framework like Bootstrap or Tailwind, and configure it to work with the React application.
- Create a new component for the expense tracker app.
- Create a form component for adding new expenses. The form should have input fields for the expense name, amount, and date.
- Create a component to display the list of expenses. Each expense item should display the name, amount, and date of the expense, and a button to delete the expense.
- Add state to the expense tracker component to manage the list of expenses.

Ctrl + Shift + Frontend

- Add logic to add new expenses to the list when the form is submitted.
- Add logic to delete expenses from the list when the delete button is clicked.
- Add logic to calculate and display the total expense amount.
- Add logic to save the list of expenses to local storage when the component unmounts, and load the list of expenses from local storage when the component mounts.

If you guys find more time you guys can add these features as well

- Add input validation for the expense form fields.
- Add sorting and filtering options for the expense list.
- Improve the UI design using the CSS framework.
- Add animations to the expense list when items are added or deleted.

Goodluck with the project guys !!

NOTE TO READERS

Dear Developers,

You did it! 🎉 Congratulations on finishing this book on web development with Angular and React! We hope you enjoyed the journey and gained some serious coding superpowers along the way. We know there were probably moments when your code just wouldn't cooperate (we've all been there), but you pushed through, and that's something to be seriously proud of!

Now that you've conquered the core concepts of web development, it's time to take things to the next level. If you've enjoyed learning with us and want to continue growing, we'd love for you to apply for internships at AiVirex Innovations LLP! We're always looking for passionate developers who are ready to dive into real-world projects and create something amazing. Think of this as your chance to turn all that knowledge into experience—and we'll be right here to help you every step of the way.

As you move forward, remember this: you're capable of greatness. You've already shown that you have the drive, the grit, and the creativity to learn and grow. Don't be afraid to experiment, make mistakes, and keep pushing boundaries—that's where the magic happens!

Thank you for spending your time with us and being a part of this amazing community. We hope this book has been as fun to read as it was for us to create. Stay curious, stay passionate, and keep coding. Who knows? Maybe one day, we'll be working on something awesome together at AiVirex.

Wishing you all the best in your web development journey!

Sincerely,
K Sai Anirudh & Hrithika R
AiVirex Innovations
Let's Innovate! ✨

www.ingramcontent.com/pod-product-compliance
Lightning Source LLC
Chambersburg PA
CBHW070147230526
45471CB00002B/558